In the name of Allah
The Merciful, the Compassionate

Presented to

....

....

GOODWORD BOOKS

Islam Rediscovered
Tell Me About the Prophet Muhammad
Tell Me About the Prophet Musa
Tell Me About the Prophet Yusuf
Tell Me About Hajj
Arabic-English Dictionary for Advanced
    Learners
A Handbook of Muslim Belief
The Moriscos of Spain
The Story of Islamic Spain
Spanish Islam (A History of the Muslims in
    Spain)
A Simple Guide to Islam's Contribution to
    Science
The Quran, Bible and Science
Islamic Medicine
Islam and the Divine Comedy
Travels of Ibn Jubayr
The Arabs in History
Decisive Moments in the History of Islam
My Discovery of Islam
Islam At the Crossroads
The Spread of Islam in the World
The Spread of Islam in France
The Islamic Art and Architecture
The Islamic Art of Persia
The Hadith for Beginners
How Greek Science Passed to Arabs
Islamic Thought and its Place in History
One Religion
Muhammad: The Hero As Prophet
A History of Arabian Music
A History of Arabic Literature
Ever Thought About the Truth?
Crude Understanding of Disbelief
The Miracle in the Ant
Allah is Known Through Reason
The Basic Concepts in the Quran
The Moral Values of the Quran
The Beautiful Commands of Allah
The Beautiful Promises of Allah
The Muslim Prayer Encyclopaedia
After Death, Life!
Living Islam: Treading the Path of Ideal
A Basic Dictionary of Islam
The Muslim Marriage Guide

A Treasury of the Quran
The Quran for All Humanity
The Quran: An Abiding Wonder
The Call of the Qur'an
Muhammad: A Prophet for All Humanity
Words of the Prophet Muhammad
An Islamic Treasury of Virtues
Islam and Peace
Introducing Islam
The Moral Vision
Principles of Islam
Indian Muslims
God Arises
Islam: The Voice of Human Nature
Islam: Creator of the Modern Age
Woman Between Islam and Western
    Society
Woman in Islamic Shari'ah
Islam As It Is
Religion and Science
Tabligh Movement
The Soul of the Quran
Presenting the Quran
The Wonderful Universe of Allah
The Quran
Selections from the Noble Reading
The Koran
Heart of the Koran
Muhammad: A Mercy to all the Nations
The Sayings of Muhammad
The Life of the Prophet Muhammad
History of the Prophet Muhammad
A-Z Steps to Leadership
The Essential Arabic
Hijab in Islam
The Way to Find God
The Teachings of Islam
The Good Life
The Garden of Paradise
The Fire of Hell
Islam and the Modern Man
Uniform Civil Code
Man Know Thyself
Muhammad: The Ideal Character
Polygamy and Islam
Concerning Divorce

A Simple Guide to™
ISLAM

FARIDA KHANAM

Goodword
B · O · O · K · S

This course has been devised to meet the requirements of the syllabus of Islamiat (introduction to Islam) of Jamia Millia Islamia, and is also recommended for general reading.

Farida Khanam has a Masters Degree in English from Delhi University and has done her Ph.D. in Islamic Studies from Jamia Millia Islamia. She is currently teaching in the Department of Islamic Studies, Jamia Millia Islamia, New Delhi.

First published by Goodword Books 2001
© Goodword Books 2002
Reprinted 2001, 2002

GOODWORD BOOKS
1, Nizamuddin West Market
New Delhi 110 013
Tel. 435 5454, 435 6666, 435 1128
Fax 435 7333, 435 7980
E-mail: skhan@vsnl.com
Website: www.alrisala.org

Contents

Introduction

"Islam" is an Arabic word which means "submission, surrender and obedience to God." In religious terms, this means that the individual who embraces Islam as his religion must put the Almighty first and foremost in his life, bowing to His wishes in all matters great and small.

Everything in the universe—the sun, the moon, the stars— have all completely subjugated themselves to His will; they cannot make the slightest deviation from the path He has ordained for them. Similarly, all other elements in nature function in obedience to the laws of nature laid down for them by their Maker. The universe, therefore, literally follows the religion of Islam in that it has surrendered to God, the Lord of the Universe.

But there is a difference between the status of man and that of the physical world. The physical world has been given no option but to submit to God, whereas man has been given free will, so that he may opt for either good or bad ways. To this end he has been given a thinking faculty, and a conscience with which to make moral judgements for himself. He has the ability to accept and reject in order to follow certain principles in life. He is not bound by fixed laws like all other created beings. He has been given freedom of thought, option and action.

It is through this liberty of choice that man is being tested. But after being given a thinking faculty, a conscience and an ability to judge between good and bad ways, he was not just left to his own resources. God did not just leave man in a world where there was no way to find the truth. Divine provision for him went much further than that. To see how God gave His guidelines to mankind, we have to go right back to the beginning of creation. He took Adam, the first man— whom He had made not just an ordinary mortal but also a prophet— and taught him everything that He wanted from man, so that human beings would not be left without proper direction or guidance. From time to time thereafter, He sent large numbers of prophets to the world— the last of these being the Prophet Muhammad— so that human beings, who tended to stray, could be recalled to the path of virtue. It is said that about one lakh twenty thousand prophets came to the world during this period.

Now the question arises as to why there was the need for such great numbers of prophets. It was because after each prophet left the world, people gradually began forgetting his teachings, till a time came when a major part of the teachings of the prophets was lost. Now in the age of the press, these teachings have been extensively published in the form of books, so that there is no fear of their being lost to succeeding generations.

Iman – Belief

The Arabic word for belief is "*Iman*." It literally means 'to know,' 'to believe,' 'to put one's trust in something or someone.' In the Islamic Shariah, *Iman* means putting one's trust in, or having complete faith in Allah, His Prophet and His message.

There are seven things which are essential for a Muslim to believe in. These come under the heading of *Iman Mufassal*, which requires a longer, more detailed declaration of faith. They are to believe in Allah, in His angels, in His revealed Book, in all of His messengers, in the Last Day (the Day of Judgement), in Taqdir, (the doctrine of predestination, which means that everything good or bad is decided by Allah), and in Life After Death.

Without *Iman*, the individual's espousal of Islam as his religion would lack credibility. That is why, if he is to be a true believer, he must not only testify to his faith by word of mouth (*Shahaada bil Lisan*), but must also accept it with all his heart and soul and then staunchly adhere to it. Furthermore, he is obliged to do good works in keeping with the fundamentals of the faith. Both belief (*iman*), and right action (*amal*) are absolutely vital.

The Shahaadah –
The Article of Faith

The Creed, or article of faith, called *Shahaadah*, literally means 'witness' or 'testimony.' The first of the five pillars of Islam, its nomenclature derives from the word '*Ashhadu*,' which means 'I declare,' or 'I bear witness.' As an Islamic term, it means testifying to faith in Islam. The words of the *Shahaada* in Arabic are: *La ilaha illa Allah Muhammad ur-rasul Allah*. This means: There is no god but Allah and Muahammad is the Messenger of Allah. Its recital is called the '*Kalimah*.'

For Muslims there are certain requirements which have to be observed regarding the *Kalimah* of *Shahaadah*. They are as follows:

> *It has to be repeated aloud, at least once in a lifetime.*

> *Its meaning has to be fully understood.*

> *It should be believed in "with the heart."*

> *It should be professed in until death.*

When spoken in Arabic and with sincerity, it is a commitment to obey God and follow the Prophet:

> *'I bear witness that there is no god but Allah; I*

bear witness that Muhammad is the Messenger of God.'

These are the first words that are breathed into a child's ear at birth. These are also the last words which a Muslim would utter with his dying breath.

Even if someone recites the *shahaadah* hypocritically—which is not acceptable to God—he will still, for practical purposes, continue to be regarded as a member of the Muslim community. Nevertheless, a proper understanding of the basic tenets is a prerequisite for all true believers. And sincere and heartfelt faith is a sine qua non if salvation is to be ensured in the life Hereafter.

The *shahaadah* consists of two parts; one, a negation, the other an affirmation. The first part— *La ilaha illa Allah* (there is no other God) negates the existence of each and every false God, and condemns false worship. The word *'ilaah'* means 'god' or any object of worship; it could refer to any being, person, matter or concept, which is taken as an object of adoration or worship.

The second part of *Shahaadah—illa Allah—* stresses that only Allah, the one and only God, the Creator and Sustainer of all being, merits our reverence. No one else is to be worshipped or turned to for help or refuge. Neither angels, nor prophets nor saints, nor any other object share in His divinity. There is only One God, One Creator, One Sustainer— the Almighty Allah,

Tawheed – The Oneness of God

Tawheed is the essence of Islam. *Tawheed* is an Arabic term which means 'oneness' and 'unity.' In Islamic terminology it means the oneness of Allah. It is a fundamental doctrine of Islam referring to the oneness of Allah in all it meanings. Thus the declaration that 'there is no God but Allah' is called *Tawheed*. Allah has no partner *(sharik)*, He exists by Himself. Nothing can rival Him as a source of power or love. There is no one worthy of worship other than Allah. He is not an abstract concept. He is always near us; He cares for us and we owe our existence to Him alone.

Islam established a close and direct relationship between the Creator and His creation. In Islam no mediating power of any kind exists between the Creator and His creation. God's absolute unity is reflected in the unity of His creation in which each individual part is in harmonious order with the remainder. There is nothing remotely like Him. The Quran thus enjoins us:

> *"Say: He is Allah, the one. Allah the Absolute. He begets not, nor is He begotten; And there is none like Him." (chapter 112).*

Tawheed means that God alone is the Creator and Sustainer of the universe including human beings. He is the only possessor of all powers. He is Omniscient, Omnipotent, and Omnipresent. That is, He knows everything, He sees everything and is present everywhere, although invisible to the naked eye.

Monotheism is to believe in the fact that all power lies in the hand of one God alone; that He alone deserves to be worshipped. No act in the nature of worship is lawful unless directed towards God. It is God alone who fulfills our needs. It is God alone who is behind the functioning of the entire universe.

Here are further verses from the Qur'an which state very clearly the concept of God:

> *"Truly your God is but one; Lord of the heavens and of the earth." (37:4)*

> *"This is God your Lord; there is no god but He, the Creator of all things; therefore, worship Him alone." (6:102)*

> *"Your God is one God; there is no God but He, the Compassionate, the Merciful (2:158)*

> *"God: there is no God but He the Living, the Eternal One. Neither slumber nor sleep overtakes Him. His is what the heavens and the earth contain. Who can intercede with Him, unless by His leave? He is cognizant of men's affairs now and in the future. Men can grasp only that part of His knowledge which He will. His throne is as vast as the heavens and the earth, and the preservation of both does not*

*weary Him. He is the Exalted, the Immense
One." (2:255)*

Tawheed has two aspects to it: *tawheed fi az-Zat* and *tawheed
fi as-Sifat*, that is, oneness of being and oneness of
attributes. This means that God is alone in His Being as
well as in His attributes.

The attributes of God are called *Al Asmaul Husna*, or the
excellent names. The Quran says: "But God's are excellent
names, call on Him thereby." (7:179) Abu Hurayrah, a
companion of the Prophet, has narrated a saying of the
Prophet to this effect: "Verily, there are ninety nine names
of God.'

Islam enjoins the believers to worship one Allah alone. No
other being or object is worthy of being worshipped. No
other being should be associated with Allah. Idolatry or
shirk is to worship or hold in reverence anything other than
God. It is strictly forbidden in Islam, and is regarded as
the worst of all sins.

THE FAR REACHING EFFECT OF TAWHEED

By believing in one true God man is saved from worshipping
many false gods. *Tawheed* enables man to establish a direct
link between God and man.

Belief in *tawheed* makes man humble and modest instead
of being proud and arrogant. It is because belief in one
Great God implies that man is His humble servant and that

modesty alone befits him. Believers know that they must submit to Allah, on whom they depend utterly. Submission to one God results in individual freedom and dignity, for, all human beings become equal and all deserve our respect. There is only one God and all of us are servants of the same God. Belief in the oneness of Allah helps individual to live in unity with others. Belief in one Creator gives a sense of oneness with all creation.

Belief in one God gives the believers confidence, for, they trust in Allah and believe that nothing can happen unless God wills it. Life and death are entirely in His hands. They remain content because they believe that power, wealth and success come from Allah alone. He gives them to whom He wants and takes them away from whom he wants. *Tawheed* thus brings about a unique blend of submission to God and human dignity and freedom.

Risalah – Prophethood

Man has been placed on this earth by God in order that his obedience to his Maker may be put to the test. For this purpose he has been given complete freedom to tread the paths of both good and evil. He has his choice. But to follow the path desired for him by God, man is in need of guiding principles. The true source of guidance, according to

Islam, is to be found in prophethood. Throughout human history, God in His infinite Mercy, has selected certain individuals to communicate His message to mankind, so that all human beings might be enabled to follow the right path. These chosen people were called prophets or messengers. They received God's message through His angel and then conveyed it to their people.

All the prophets, according to Islam, brought the same basic truth: that there is only one God and that all human beings are accountable to God for their actions: when Doomsday finally comes, they will be judged by Him according to their good and bad deeds. Those who believe in Allah and His Prophet shall be rewarded by God in the next world. While those who disbelieve shall be punished by God in the next world according to the deeds they have performed on earth.

> *"Allah chooses to Himself whom He will, and guides to Himself those that repent." (42:13)*

God's messengers came in every age and to every region. According to a *hadith*, starting with Adam and ending with the Prophet Muahmmad ﷺ 1,24,000 messengers were sent to guide the people to the right path. The prophets mentioned by name in the Qur'an are two dozen in number. The five major prophets who came before Muhammad ﷺ were Adam, Nuh, (Noah) Ibrahim, (Abraham) Musa (Moses) and Isa (Jesus). The Prophet Muhammad ﷺ, the last in this long line of prophets, was known as the 'seal of the Prophet.'

In the past the need for new prophets had arisen because God's religion was no longer in its pristine form, having been distorted in a number of different ways. New prophets had to come to the world periodically in order to revive the true spirit of religion, and thus restore it to its original form. After the Prophet Muhammad, there was no need for another prophet, for the Book— the Qur'an— which he gave to the world has been preserved intact, in its original form.

The Islamic concept of prophethood is different from that of other religions. Some religions would have it that even God Himself becomes incarnate in human shape, and that his prophets are in some way superhuman or otherworldly. But a prophet in the Islamic sense is no different from any other human being. His uniqueness lies simply in his being the chosen messenger of God.

God's Apostles were born into this world just like any other human beings. They led their lives just as others did, thus demonstrating to their people how God's servants should, in practice, conduct themselves on earth and showing them clearly what path they must tread in order to avert God's displeasure and be worthy of His blessings.

The prophets who brought books were called *rasul*, while those who did not were called *nabi*.

Of the holy books, four find mention in the Qur'an: the *Sahifa*, scrolls given to Ibrahim; the *Tawrat*, the revelations to Musa; the *Zabur*, the psalms given to Dawud (David); the *Injil*, the teachings given to Isa (Jesus). Each of these was originally a complete revelation, but unfortunately, these books and teachings were not properly preserved. Some, like the *Sahifa*, were lost completely. Others were changed in various ways by human intervention. Thus these previous scriptures are no longer in their original form. They could best be described as edited versions of divine revelations, which have been altered from time to time by editors and commentators. Since these holy scriptures are no longer in their original form.

Malaika – Angels

Angels (*malak*, literally meaning 'messenger') serve as intermediaries between God and man. They transmit messages to His envoys, worthy individuals who are specially chosen by God for the task of being His messengers. These messengers are called prophets, and it is the prophets alone who receive the divine revelations, through an angel, who is the celestial messenger. According to the Qur'an, the angel Jibrail (Gabriel), meaning the 'power of God,' — also alluded to in the Qur'an as a "trustworthy spirit" (*al-ruh-al-amin*)—brought divine revelations to the Prophet of Islam.

Most important among the angels are Jibrail, Mikail, Izrail and Israfil.

Jibrail, as we have said, is the 'holy spirit', who brings revelations from Allah to His prophets.

Izrail is called the angel of death, for he takes away the souls of the dying.

Israfil will blow the trumpet when the time comes for the world to end and on the Day of Judgement.

The angels, who continuously praise and glorify the Lord, have been given the necessary qualities and powers to perform specific functions. They have no free will. They always obey Allah and never displease Him. Man, on the other hand, has been given free will and can choose between right and wrong.

Angels are creatures of light (*Nur*) who pervade the whole universe. Although in the kingdom of Allah there are many millions of them, they belong to the realm of the invisible, so that the only way that we can see them is if they appear in human form. Jibrail used to appear to the Prophet in various forms. Sometimes he hung suspended in the air, sometimes he appeared in the shape of a man, and sometimes he sprouted wings, etc. The angel Jibrail once appeared before a gathering of the companions of the

Prophet in order to teach them about Islam. On that occasion, he took the form of a companion of the Prophet. Angels can take any suitable form in order to perform their duties, and are constantly occupied in carrying out Allah's orders.

Angels are continuously present on earth, particularly at moments of prayers. Man may not be able to see the angels, but the angels can certainly see man and are in constant touch with human beings. They keep a watch on them on behalf of God and many of them are eternally busy recording all of our thoughts, words and deeds. They are called the 'respected recorders' (*kiraman katibin*). Not a single word we say goes unrecorded. (50:18)

They are the friends and protectors (41:30-32) of human beings, and are God's most obedient and loyal servants.

Ma'ad – Life after Death

According to Islam, the present world is not an eternal abode. The Qur'an tells us that man is placed here only temporarily, so that his moral fibre may be tested in terms of his obedience to God's will. He must always remember that there will be the life hereafter, or *Akhirat* as it is known in Islamic terminology. This is also referred to as *Ma'ad*, which means a place to which one returns.

There is a time limit to mortal existence. Death marks the end of the testing period for all human beings. But death only means a change of abode, for the soul never dies. Man returns to the realm whence he came, so that he may wait for Judgement Day. That realm, the life hereafter, is the eternal world. Thus man's life is divided into two parts: a brief stay in this world and an eternal life in the next world. To the ungodly, it is only then that it becomes obvious that a life which is eternal is far more important than this present existence.

God created human beings and made them responsible for their actions by granting them freedom. If there were no Afterlife in which the good were rewarded and the bad punished, there would be no justice; in which case, it would appear meaningless to create people with a conscience and a sense of responsibility. But God is just and always acts justly. Hence it is the absolute demand of justice that there should be a Day of Judgement on which everyone is brought to book.

After death, human beings will, therefore, leave this present, ephemeral abode and, on the Day of Judgement, will enter another world, which will be eternal. When the time comes for the Last Reckoning, God will destroy this world and replace it with a permanent, everlasting world. All human beings will then be resurrected and brought before the Almighty to be judged. On that day, everyone will stand alone before God. Those who have done good deeds in the world they have left behind will be rewarded. Their

reward will be paradise, a state of joy, happiness and peace.

The Qur'an states: "Allah has created death and life to test which one of you is best in conduct." (67:1)

Death is not the end of our lives; it is the beginning of our real life. Because our future fate is being decided on the basis of our present performance, we can either make use of our opportunities on earth to ensure a well-deserved place for ourselves in Paradise, or we can throw them away and condemn ourselves to punishment in Hell.

The belief in the Hereafter naturally has a great influence on the life of a believer. When he knows that Allah is watching all his actions, his behaviour will be responsible. He will always endeavour to lead his life in consonance with the will of God and will inevitably avoid any course which will incur God's displeasure.

Furthermore, the concept of the Hereafter gives a fuller meaning and purpose to the life of the believer. One who firmly believes in this concept will not give in to greed and other such worldly failings. He will not be a materialist, for he knows that this material life will surely come to an end with death, whereas there will be a whole eternity before him in the Afterlife, during which he will certainly rejoice in having paid due attention to the spiritual side of life on this earth.

Taqdir – Predestination

Taqdir (predestination) forms part of the fundamental beliefs of Islam. This is the sixth article of faith. *Taqdir* in Arabic is also called *Al-Qadha-o-al Qadr*, which means to "measure out" or "pre-ordering."

Taqdir means belief in God's having for all eternity, predetermined and decreed all things, good as well as bad. Nothing can happen of itself in the world, good or evil. God has created this universe with His Power, His knowledge, His wisdom and His will and has set for it a certain course. Then He has ordained a law, which may be called the law of nature, for the physical, animal and human world. Everything in this universe. The Qur'an says:

> *"The Lord has created and balanced all things and has fixed their destinies and guided them."*
> *(87:2)*

Nothing can befall us but what God has destined for us.

> *"We have created all things according to a fixed decree." (54:49)*

For all of His creation God has set a course to follow. Nothing can deviate from the path set by God. In this respect the movements of the sun, moon, the stars and planets, the rotation of the earth, the laws of cause and effect working behind the growth and function of all natural phenomena the existence of all living creatures including human beings, their life and death—all are governed by natural laws. In religious terminology this is the divine *taqdir*.

The belief in *taqdir* is to acknowledge that God's power is limitless. His Decree is eternal. No one can come in the way of fulfilling His decrees. His knowledge is eternal. That is, whatever happens, is happening, or is to happen in future, is in the knowledge of God beforehand. Nothing pertaining to the past, present or future is concealed from His view .He is abreast of all the minutest details of this universe. Everything that has been or will be depends entirely on His foreknowledge and sovereign will.

There is some misunderstanding about this belief in *taqdir*. There are certain people who believe that man is totally helpless. This is not true. There is no doubt about it that it is what God decrees which takes place. No one can change His *taqdir*. But it is also true that man has been granted by God wisdom, freedom and will power. This is quite exceptional, for the rest of the objects of the universe have not been granted any free will; they have to follow the path set for them by God. But the case of man is different. He has been given the power of discrimination between good and bad. Then he has also been granted the freedom to choose one course and leave another. For instance, according to Islam, just as disease is a *taqdir* of God, so is its remedy. Therefore, if one falls ill he may counter it with the other *taqdir* of God, that is he may take medicine for it. Similarly, good or evil both are God's *taqdir*. Now man has the freedom to opt for whatever *taqdir* he think fit.

Salat – Prayer

Salat is the second pillar of Islam. It is the duty of every adult Muslim to perform the five daily prayers individually or in congregation. In the case of missed prayers, we can make up for them later. For *salat* to be acceptable to God, it should be performed at the proper time, in purity, facing the *qiblah* or the direction of the Ka'bah.

These five obligatory prayers have to be observed at fixed times. Allah says in the Qur'an:

> "Salat *at fixed times has been enjoined on the believers."* (4:103)

The five daily prayers are:

1. Early morning prayer: two rakas. Its period is between dawn and sunrise.

2. Noon prayer: Four rakas, between noon and mid-afternoon.

3. Afternoon prayer: Four rakas between the time when the shadow begins to become equal.

4. Sunset prayer: Three rak'as, between sunset and early evening.

5. Evening prayer: Four rak'as from the disappearance of twilight until dawn.

6. Friday prayer: Two rak'as to be performed following the sermon. They have to be performed in congregation in a mosque. In the absence of these conditions this prayer has to be replaced by the midday (noon) prayer.

The five daily prayers were made obligatory for Muslims on the occasion of Miraj (the Prophet's heavenly journey) This is very significant. For the Prophet has been recorded as having said that 'through the services of worship a believer reaches his own ascension, that he is raised into the presence of God. If a believer performs *salat* in its proper spirit he will be blessed with a spiritual experience which will make him feel that he has come closer to God.

The following is the way prayer is performed. First of all the believer performs ablutions. Then he stands up in the right direction facing towards the Ka'bah in Makkah. He then holds up his hands, speaking aloud: "God alone is great." Then submits himself to the will of His Lord alone.

After praising Him by reciting some passages from the Qur'an, he begins to feel the majesty of God. Then he prostrates himself touching his forehead to the ground. Self-prostration is in acknowledgment of the majesty of God.

Muslims have been advised in the Qur'an to be steadfast in their prayer, (29:45) for prayer keeps away indecency and evil. When the Prophet of Islam was asked about this verse he said: If a person's prayer does not keep him away from indecency and evil then his prayer is not really prayer at all.

How does prayer become the means of inculcating these virtues in the faithful? It is because prayers remind us five times daily, that we are living before a God who is watching us. One who performs his prayer in its true spirit cannot become forgetful of God after his prayer is over. The actions of prayer are a manifestation of the fact that one's heart is full of fear and love for God. Therefore, if one prays in the true spirit of prayer, one's prayer will surely fend off indecency and evil.

The aims of *salah* are:

1. to bring people closer to God.

2. to keep human beings from indulging in indecent, shameful and forbidden activities.

3. to purify the heart, develop the mind and comfort the soul.

4. to remind people constantly of God and His greatness.

5. to develop discipline and will power.

6. to guide people to the most upright way of life.

7. to show equality, unity and brotherhood.

8. to promote patience, courage, hope, and confidence.

9. to train people in cleanliness, purity and punctuality.

10. to develop gratitude and humility.

11. to demonstrate obedience to our Creator.

Zakat – Almsgiving

Zakat, or the alms-tax, is the third pillar of Islam. There are two forms of charity in Islam—obligatory and voluntary which are called *zakat* and *sadaka* respectively. *Zakat* means (to purify) from the verb zakah. By giving up of a portion of the wealth in one's possession, the remainder is purified or legalised to be used by the alms-giver.

Zakat is God's due portion of what we own and what we produce. There are many ways of making a living in this world: one can work on the land, in a factory, a shop or in an office. But what part do we actually play in all this? Our role is, in fact, minimal. Multiple forces are at work in the universe and within ourselves, which accord to our needs. All these forces come together to enable us to earn a livelihood. All this has been ordained by the Lord of the Universe. That is why, once a year, one should calculate one's earnings, and put aside a portion for God. In so doing, one acknowledges the fact that it is all from God.

Without His help, one could earn nothing. To spend for the cause of God is to express a sublime attachment to the Lord; it shows a yearning to empty oneself before him. One should feel as one gives that one is offering everything to God and seeking nothing for oneself. This is the spirit in which a Muslim should help others:

> *We feed you for God's sake only; we seek of you neither recompense nor thanks. (76:9)*

Eight categories of people, eligible to receive *Zakat*, have been specified in this verse of the Qur'an:

> *"Alms shall be used only for the advancement of God's cause, for the ransom of captives and debtors, and for distribution among the poor, the destitute, wayfarers, those that are employed in collecting alms, and those that are converted to the faith. This is a duty enjoined by God. He is Wise and All-Knowing." (9:60)*

Zakat funds are to be spent, according to the Qur'an, on the poor and the destitute, the wayfarer, the bankrupt, the needy, converts, captives, collectors of *Zakat* and in the cause of God. The last category allows Zakat funds to be used for the general welfare of the community— for education of the people, for public works, and for any other need of the Muslim community. *Zakat* in spirit is an act of worship, while in its external form, it is the carrying out of a social service.

Zakat is thus not merely the payment of a tax, as it is generally understood. It has indeed a great religious significance. Its importance is underscored by the fact that the Qur'an treats it at par with *salat* (prayer). The Qur'an frequently enjoins the believers, 'to perform the worship and pay the *Zakat*.' The Qur'an goes to the extent of saying that one cannot attain righteousness unless one spends out of one's wealth for the love of God. In the words of the Qur'an:

> *"By no means shall you attain righteousness*
> *unless you give of that which you love." (3:92)*

> *The Qur'an disapproves of people who make a*
> *show of their alms-giving. (2:271)*

Zakat is a test of the sincerity and unselfishness of the believer. For there is no authority to force any Muslim to pay it. It is entirely up to the conscience of the individual whether or not he or she pays it. The willingness to pay, shows that one's heart is clean of the love of money. It shows that one is prepared to use one's money for the service of humanity.

The Prophet of Islam was always very concerned for the poor and the needy. He went to the extent of saying:

He is not a believer who eats his fill while his neighbour remains hungry by his side. (Muslim).

Sawm – Fasting of Ramadan

Sawm, or ritual fasting is the third pillar of Islam. Fasting is prescribed once a year during Ramadan, the 9th month of the Islamic Calendar. The fast of Ramadan lasts for the whole month beginning from sunrise and ending at sunset God Almighty says: "You who believe! Fasting is prescribed for you as it was prescribed for those before you that you may (learn) self - restraint" (2:183).

Fasting means to refrain and abstain from dawn till sunset, from food and drink and certain other things. Fasting in the month of Ramadan begins with the sighting of the new moon, and it ends with the sighting of the moon of the next month of Shawwal. With the new moon of Ramadan fasting becomes obligatory my for all those who are required to fast. With the new moon of Shawwal the fast comes to an end. The following day is the day of celebration of Id festival.

If one is sick or on a journey, one is allowed to postpone fast. But the missed fast has to be made up by fasting the same number of days afterwards.

The fast teaches discipline to the soul. The believer recalls the month in which the first verses of the Quran were revealed.

According to the Qur'an, the main purpose of fasting is to attain taqwa or God-consciousness. Fasting, according to the Prophet, is a shield, which guards us from evil ways.

In Ramadan extra salat is performed. There are extra sunnah salat on Ramazan nights called salat at- Tarawih. In the last ten days of Ramadan, some retreat to the mosque to perform Itikaaf, to pray and to read the Qur'an as much as they can.

Ramadan is a blessed month. The Qur'an was revealed in this month. Ramadan is also called the month of the Quran.

BENEFITS OF FASTING

1. All Muslims, rich and poor, fulfill the same demands of the fast and then share their food together at night. This promotes the spirit of togetherness.

2. The rich gain a better understanding of what it must be like for the poor who cannot always eat when they want to. This should make them more generous towards them.

3. Muslims learn to appreciate .all the good things they have each day, and to thank Allah for them, instead of just taking them for granted.

4. Muslims learn self control.

5. Muslims learn how to endure hardship.

Ramadan thus brings us closer to the path of goodness and God-consciousness (taqwa). Ramadan thus brings us closer to God.

FASTING AT TIMES OTHER THAN RAMADAN

Fasting in Islam is undertaken more often than simply during Ramadan. The notion of *kaffara*, atonement for sin or for duties which have been omitted, is stipulated in the Qur'an on a number of occasions: in chapter 2/196, fasting is to replace the pilgrimage for those unable to go to Mecca under certain conditions; in Qur'an 5/89, fasting is prescribed for breaking an oath; in Qur'an 5/95, fasting is the penalty for killing an animal while on the hajj. In each of these situations, fasting is seen as making amends for one's moral or ritual errors.

Additional fasting is also practised on the ninth and tenth of Muharram; during the six days from the second to the seventh of shawwal and on the ninth of Dhu al Hijja for those who are not on pilgrimage. Additional fasting is also observed on the twenty seventh of Rajab, the fifteenth of Sha'aban and three days of every month of the lunar calendar.

Hajj – The Pilgrimage

Hajj, pilgrimage, is one of the five pillars of Islam. The Prophet observed: "There are five basic pillars of Islam. To bear testimony that there is no deity save Allah, and that Muhammad is His Prophet; to say prayers regularly and pay the poor-due; to make a pilgrimage to the house of God, and fast during Ramadan."

The root meaning of the word *"Hajj"* is "to set out" or to make a pilgrimage. Canonically it has come to refer to a Muslim act of worship, performed annually in the month of Zul Hijjah, the twelfth month of the lunar calendar.

To perform *Hajj* is incumbent at least once in a lifetime, upon every Muslim, who is an adult, free, in good health and has sufficient money for the expenses of the journey. Women have to be accompanied by a close relative (*maharam*) like a husband, father, son or brother.

There are two types of pilgrimage— *Umrah* and *Hajj*. *Umrah* is called the lesser pilgrimage. To perform *Umrah*, one visits the Ka'bah at any time of the year other than *Hajj* time.

But the performance of *Hajj* has to be made during the dates fixed for it. Three months, called the Hajj months, are — *Shawwal, Dhul Qadah, Dhul Hijjah*— the 10th, 11th and 12th months of the Islamic calender.

The pilgrims begin their journey in *Shawwal* but the rituals of *Hajj* are performed only from the 8th to the 12th *Dhul Hijjah*.

There are a number of important rites, to be performed during the *Hajj*

1. *Niyyah:* The pilgrim expresses the intention of performing *Hajj*.

2. *Ihram:* After cleaning himself, the pilgrim puts on the special dress called *Ihram,* a white seamless garment, by wearing which he enters the state of *Ihram*.

3. *Talbiya:* After putting on *Ihram* the pilgrim recites the *talbiya:* "I stand up for your service O God! I stand up! I

stand up! There is no partner with You! I stand up! Truly Yours is the Praise, the Blessing and the Sovereignty. There is no partner with You."

The *talbiya* continues until the throwing of stones.

4. *Tawaf:* going round the Ka'bah seven times. Seven times at arrival in Makkah and seven times on the 10th *Dhul Hijjah*, after sacrificing an animal.

5. *Saee:* the pilgrim undertakes a fast walk between Safa and Marwah, two hillocks near the Ka'bah.

There are a number of other rites to be performed during the Hajj:

— Standing on Arafat: The pilgrims gather in Arafat and pray to God throughout the day, reciting the *talbiyya*. This standing on the 9th day of *Dhul Hijjah* is very important According to a tradition, standing on Arafat is the culmination of the pilgrimage. The pilgrims leave Arafat after sunset:

— to stay in Muzdalifah;

— to perform the casting of the stones at three pillars symbolizing the devil.

— to shave the head or shorten their hair after the pilgrimage is over. Females only trim their hair;

— finally an animal is sacrificed and the pilgrim returns to perform the farewell *tawaf* of the Ka'bah. Now the pilgrimage is complete.

The pilgrimage ends with the Feast of Sacrifice, *Eid al Adha*. The pilgrim then visits the Prophet's mosque in Madinah.

Among all Muslim acts of worship, *Hajj* holds a prominent position. In one Hadith, the Prophet called it "the supreme act of worship." But it is not just the rites of pilgrimage that constitute this importance, it is the spirit in which Hajj is performed. Let us put this another way and say that it is not merely a matter of going to Makkah and returning. There is much more to *hajj* than that. *Hajj* has been prescribed so that it may inspire us with a new religious fervour. To return from *Hajj* with one's faith in God strengthened and rekindled— that is the hallmark of a true pilgrim. *Hajj* assumes a supreme act of worship when it is undertaken in its true spirit, and performed in the proper manner. It will then be the greatest act in a pilgrim's life: he will never be the same again.

To go on the Hajj is to meet God. When the pilgrim reaches *Meeqat,* the border of the Sacred Territory, he is filled with awe of God: he feels that he is leaving his own world, and entering God's. Now he is touching the Lord, revolving around Him, running towards Him, journeying on His behalf, making a sacrifice in His name, praying to the Lord and seeing his prayers answered.

The House of God in Makkah is one of God's signs on earth. The souls which have strayed from the Lord take comfort in Him once again; hearts which have become hard as stone are brought low before Almighty God; eyes which have lost their vision are filled with divine radiance. But these blessings of *Hajj* are available only to those who come prepared for them. Otherwise *Hajj* will be just a tour, a visit which leaves no lasting impression upon the traveller.

The pilgrims gather on the plain of Arafat in order to recall the time when they will gather on the plain of the Last Day. They conjure up visions in this world of what they will experience in practice in the next world.

The Prophet Muhammad said: "*Hajj* is to stand in the plains of *Arafat*." This shows how important it is to visit Arafat and to spend time there. The plain of Arafat, where the pilgrims spend one whole day is like a picture of the Day of Reckoning. Believers come in from all sides to witness the spectacle. All are clad in a simple garment. There is nothing to make anyone stand out from the rest. All recite the same words: "Here we are at your service, Lord." Anyone who sees this spectacle must be reminded of this verse from the Qur'an:

> "And with one blast of the trumpet all shall rise
> from their graves and gather before Us." (36:51)

For all these reasons, *Hajj* reigns supreme among all acts of devotion. Just as the Sacred Mosque in Makkah has a station above all other mosques, so the worship that is performed there— as part of the pilgrimage— stands head and shoulders above all other acts of devotion.

Muhammad – The Prophet of Islam

Muhammed ﷺ meaning the praised one was born in 571 in the North Arabian city of Makkah, which was then inhabited mainly by the tribe of Quraysh. In those times, this tribe enjoyed throughout Arabia and the neighbouring countries great prestige on account of the position of their city as a flourishing trade and religious centre.

Their caravans, which journeyed to Syria and Yaman, and the most ancient shrine of Kabah at Makkah annually drew a great number of Arabian pilgrims. Though most of the Arabians were then idol-worshippers, several other religions, including Christianity and Judaism, had followers in Arabia. But none of those other religions could claim to have been at any time the religion of more than a negligible minority.

Muhammad's family belonged to one of the noble clans of Quraysh—the clan of Banu Hashim. He grew up as an orphan. His father Abdullah died before he was born and his mother Amina died when he was six years old. It fell first to his grandfather Abdul Muttalib to take care of him and then to his uncle Abu Talib. As from his early youth he impressed his countrymen as a person of high integrity, and they called him the trustworthy (Al-Ameen).

When Muhammad ﷺ was twenty five years old, he married Khadija, a wealthy and noble widow who had engaged him to handle her caravan trade and who had developed great admiration and respect for his noble character.

Khadija was very broadminded and understanding. Khadija being a very wealthy lady, Prophet now had all the opportunity to lead a happy, contented life. But Prophet was a truth-seeker. He was not content with the pleasures of this material world. so he would retire for days to a cave called Hira on a hill near Makkah for meditation and spiritual devotion. When in 610 A.D. he received his Divine call in that cave Khadija was the first to recognize him as the Apostle of Allah and to convert to Islam. She remaining until her death in 620 A.D. a source of comfort and support to him. She gladly spent all her wealth in the cause of Islam.

In the fortieth year of his life, one day, while he was sitting in-the solitude of the cave, an angel of God appeared before him in human shape, and addressed him with the words of God:

> *"Announce in the name of thy Lord, that He*
> *hath created, created man from a clot—*

Announce! And they Lord is most generous.
Who hath afforded knowledge through the pen,
afforded man the Knowledge of what he knew
not..." (Quran, 96:1-5)

The Prophet had found the answers to his questions. "Have We not broadened thy heart for thee, and relieved thee of thy burden which had weighed down thy back ..." (The Quran 94: 1-3) His restless soul was now in communion with the Lord of the Universe. God now chose him as His special envoy and gave him guidance. The Revelation of God began descending upon him and continued to do so for twenty three years, at the end of which time, the last Scripture of God, the Quran, reached completion.

In the twelfth year of his mission the Prophet was taken to heavens, this journey is known as Miraj (ascent). The Quran has referred to this event in the chapter entitled: Al-Isra (The Night Journey) "Praise be to Him who carried his servant by night from the Masjidul Haram (Kabah) to the Masjidul Aqsa (Jerusalem)".

Muhammad's career as Prophet lasted for about 23 years, about half of which he spent in Makkah and the rest in Madinah, which lies about 280 miles north of Makkah. During the first period, his efforts to win the Makkans to Islam met with vehement opposition, and in 622 A.D. he had to emigrate, along with the few followers he had been able to convert, to Madinah. Here the Prophet was given a hearty welcome, and moved from one sucess to another. By the time he died in 632 A.D. he had united all Arabia under the banner of Islam and completed his message to mankind.

THE ETHICAL ASPECT OF THE LIFE OF THE PROPHET

"Verily in the messenger of God, you have a good example" (33:21)

The brightest aspect of the prophet's life is that he always did what he said. There was not an injunction revealed to him that he did not demonstrate by his own example. He talked about faith, the unity of God, prayer, fasting, pilgrimage, poor-due, charity, struggle for the cause of God, self-sacrifice, patience, endurance, thanksgiving, virtuous deeds, and demonstrated every one of these by setting a personal example. His life thus became an illustration of what is written in the Qur' an. Once a few Companions asked Ayesha about the moral virtues of the Prophet. She replied, "Have you not read the Qur'an? He was a personification of the Qur'an." The Qur'an thus contains precepts in words and phrases, while prophet Muhammad's life is their practical demonstration.

'A' isha, the Prophet's wife, who had spent nine years of her life with the Prophet, affirms: "He never spoke ill of anybody. Instead of returning evil for evil, he used to forgive those who gave offence to him. He never sought revenge. He never hit any maid or slave or servant, or even a dumb creature. He never turned down a seemly request whosoever made it."

Among the relatives of the Prophet, nobody was closer to him than Ali. He had been with the Prophet from his childhood. He bears witness that the Prophet was of cheerful disposition, kindhearted and had a clear conscience. He was never harsh to anybody. If he disliked to request made by someone, he normally kept quiet instead of giving a blunt reply. Those who knew his habits, understood what he meant by his silence. He never liked to sadden anybody, rather, he used to set people's hearts at ease. He was kind, and compassionate.

It was a pleasure to have his company. Whoever met him for the first time was filled with awe, but, on closer contact, became attached to him.

According to the French philosopher, Voltaire (1694-1778), "No one is a hero to his valet." The reason for this is that a valet has access to a person's private life, and in private life no one is perfect. Those close to a person usually do not hold him in such high esteem as those who are further off. That is why they cannot come to think of him as a hero. But as Soren Smith has written, this does not hold true for the Prophet of Islam. History shows that the closer one came to him, the more one was taken by his fine qualities.

Here are a few incidents which illustrate that the Prophet of Islam always practised what he preached to others.

Once when the Prophet was at home with his wife, Umm Salamah, he summoned the maidservant for some errand, but she seemed to take a long time in coming, Seeing signs of anger on the Prophet's face Umm Salamah got up to see what had happened to the girl. She opened the curtain and saw her playing outside with the goat's kids. She called to her once again, and this time she came. The Prophet was holding a tooth-stick at the time, "If I had not feared the retribution of Judgement Day, he said to the girl, "I would have hit you with this tooth-stick."

It happened that a woman of Madinah, who used to clean the mosque, passed away. She was black-skinned and mentally deranged and there were few to perform her funeral. Those who came to it did not think it proper to inform the Prophet. When he finally heard about it, he asked to be informed of the death of any Muslim in future, irrespective of his or her status. And he performed the funeral service later.

At the Battle of Uhud, the Prophet had his teeth broken by a stone thrown at him by one of the enemy, and blood streamed from his mouth. Some of the Companions urged the Prophet to curse these enemies who wrought such havoc. (Among the many Companions who died in the battle was the Prophet's own uncle Hamzah). The Prophet's response to this was: "I have not been sent as a curse. I have been sent as a preacher and the bearer of God's mercy."

Whatever the dish brought before the Prophet, he would never say anything disparaging about it. According to Abu

Hurayrah the Prophet was never in the habit of finding fault with food. If he liked something, he ate it; if not, he left it.

Anas ibn Malik tells of how, once, when he and the Prophet, who was garbed in a thick-bordered Abyssinian shawl, were walking along together when they came across a man of rustic appearance, who came up to them and caught hold of the Prophet's shawl. He pulled at it with such force that marks apeared on the Prophet's neck." O Mohammad, give me some of God's wealth which is in your keeping," said the man. Quite unaffected by the man's rudeness, the Prophet smiled and gave orders for him to be provided for from the Treasury according to his needs.

An important statement which the Prophet made once concerned the special moments that there should be in the lives of the God-fearing:

There should be:

> *Moments when one should commune with God,*

> *Moments when one should be one's own assessor,*

> *Moments when one should be reflecting upon the mysteries of creation,*

> *And also moments for the acquisition of the necessities of life.*

Adopting a high code of ethics means practising what one

preaches; treating the weak with the same courtesy and deference as one shows to the strong; setting the same standards for oneself as one sets for others. From this point of view, the Prophet of Islam stood at the pinnacle of human ethics, never abandoning the lofty standards that he preached. And no testimony to this superior moral life he lead is more reliable than that of his closest companions.

Pious Caliphate

The first four caliphs are known as the rightly guided caliphs. They were successors of the Prophet in the real sense of the word. They were all senior companions of the Prophet. They were chosen by the Muslims for their closeness to the Prophet and for their outstanding character. They were humble, unselfish, tolerant, God-fearing and well-versed in the Quran. They remained in close touch with the people. They refused to take any luxuries for themselves.

Masters of a vast empire they continued to lead simple lives just as the Prophet had done. During the 30 years of their rule Islam made great progress. This period of Islamic rule is the golden period of justice and fair play. That is why these caliphs are called rightly guided, for they ruled the people of their time exactly in accordance with the teachings of the Quran and the Sunnah of the Prophet. They considered themselves as simple servants of God.

ABU BAKR AS-SIDDIQ - THE FIRST CALIPH (632-34)

Abu Bakr was a rich merchant of Makkah, belonging to the Quraysh tribe. At the time when Muhammad ﷺ was endowed with prophethood, Abu Bakr had gone to Yaman on business. When he came back, people immediately came to him to give him the 'strange' news of Muhammad receiving revelations from Gabriel. Having been the Prophet's close friend since boyhood (born in Makkah in 573 A.D., he was just three years younger than the Prophet), Abu Bakr was too keenly aware of the sincerity and truthfulness of the Prophet to have any misgivings.

However, on hearing this news, Abu Bakr went to see the Prophet, and asked him about the message of this religion that he was preaching. Having unshakeable faith in the Prophet, he accepted Islam without any second thoughts. That is why he was given the title As Siddiq (the upright) by the Prophet. He was thus the first male convert to Islam, and was one of the Prophet's oldest supporters. Abu Bakr's father, Uthman, (better known as Abu Qahafa) and his mother, Salma, had named him Abdul Kaaba, meaning "the servant of the Kaaba". But when he embraced Islam, the Prophet changed this pagan name to Abdullah and gave him the surname of Abu Bakr.

Even prior to Islam Abu Bakr had been respected for his good moral character. He was honest and truthful and had good relations with everyone. The Quraysh trusted him and consulted him for solutions to their problems. Now, after having accepted Islam, he began to spread the word of Allah in his own social circle. As a result of his efforts, some very promising and talented people accepted Islam, most of whom were his friends. They were — Usman ibn Affan, Zubayr ibn Al Awam, Abdur Rahman ibn Auf, Saad ibn Abi Waqqas, Abu Ubaydah ibn Al Jarrah, Khalid ibn Sayeed, etc.

When the Quraysh came to know of his role in the spread of Islam, they turned against him and began to persecute him. But he patiently bore all their oppression, and faithfully stood by the Prophet amidst all dangers. He spent all his wealth in the cause of Islam.

It was because of his sincerity and dedication to the cause of Islam that the Prophet chose him to accompany him when he migrated from Makkah to Madinah. His self-sacrificing friendship and his devotion to the cause of Islam was rewarded by his name being immortalized in the Quran as "the second of the two." (9:40)

In obedience to a divine injunction, the Muslims then left their hearth and home for Madinah. But the Quraysh did not allow them to rest in peace even in Madinah. They waged many battles in their bid to uproot the Muslims from the city. Abu Bakr took part in all these battles. He was always with the Prophet and accompanied him on all his campaigns. He never showed any weakness, always standing like a rock by the side of the Prophet.

Tabuk was the last expedition of the Prophet of Islam. He asked people to give generously in aid of it. Abu Bakr was the only person to give all he had to the cause of Islam. The Prophet asked him whether he had anything left for his wife and children. He replied that Allah and His apostle were enough for them. No one could surpass him so far as selfless service to Islam was concerned. Not only was he the first man to accept Islam, but he was also the foremost among the Muslims to uphold the cause of Allah.

After Makkah was conquered, the Prophet sent Abu Bakr in 631 to Makkah to lead the Hajj on behalf of the Prophet. Abu Bakr read the sermon (Khutba) of Hajj.

Ever since the Prophet had come to Madinah, he had been in the habit of leading the prayer himself. During his last illness the Prophet became so weak that he could not come to the mosque for this purpose. The Prophet then asked Abu Bakr to conduct the prayer in the mosque and to lead the Muslims in his stead. Aisha, who was Abu Bakr's daughter and the wife of the Prophet, thought that her tender-hearted father would not be able to bear this burden. She therefore requested the Prophet to ask someone else to perform this duty. But the Prophet did not change his mind.

Thus, in the lifetime of the Prophet, Abu Bakr came to fill the highest office. This distinction made it possible for Umar and his friends, after the Prophet's death in 632, to propose Abu Bakr as the head of the community. Abu Bakr thus became Caliph (the successor of the Prophet) by the general consent of the people.

Thanks to his simple but firm character, he was able to lead the young Muslim community successfully through the most difficult times. After the death of the Prophet, a number of the Arab tribes revolted. Most of them had embraced Islam after the conquest of Makkah in A.H. 8. and had not had the opportunity to undergo any proper training by the Prophet. Being used to a free and easy life, they found such Islamic injunctions as zakat and jihad more that they could tolerate. They were under the impression that, after the Prophet, God's succour too had come to an end.

But Abu Bakr did not let the situation get out of hand. He dealt with them firmly, having chosen the brave general Khalid ibn al Walid as the commander of his forces. He managed to suppress all revolts and brought all the Arabian tribes under the control of Islam.

Abu Bakr treated the vanquished mercifully. This helped to re-establish peace in the country. Arabia was brought under control within less than a year. Later, Abu Bakr sent Khalid and other able generals on a campaign against Persia and Byzantine.

By resorting to these measures Abu Bakr very successfully brought about much-needed unity among the Muslim community. During his short rule, the Arabian army saw several victories. Al-Hira in Persia was conquered in 633.

Soon after, Abu Bakr took ill in 13 A.H. On his death bed what Abu Bakr feared more than anything was division among the Muslims. He wanted to make sure that no difference should divide them after he was gone. After much thought, he decided to nominate Umar as his successor.. When he put his choice before the senior companions, they all approved of it. When all of the companions had agreed to this, he went ahead with the nomination.

Abu Bakr passed away two weeks after the appointment of Umar. According to his wish, he was buried by the side of the Prophet, and his body was wrapped in the same old clothes in which he had died. His rule had lasted for two years and three months.

Abu Bakr had lived a very simple and modest life. He had had neither servants nor bodyguards. He used to come early in the morning to the Prophet's mosque to carry out the duties of the state and to perform the congregational prayers. He even did routine chores at home, sweeping the floor, feeding and milking the goats, etc.

Abu Bakr lived and worked for Islam till his last breath. Although his rule lasted only for two years, three months and ten days — a very short span of time for a nation — he had been able to perform great feats. One of the many great contributions made by Abu Bakr was the collection and collation of the Quran in codex form. His achievements have rendered his name immortal.

Umar ibn Khattab, the second Caliph is the founder of the Arab empire. He was born in pagan Makkah. He was converted to Islam by his sister Fatimah, four years before the migration to Madina. He was completely opposed to the Prophet at first. He had actually set out to kill him. But on his way someone told him that his sister and her husband had become Muslims. On hearing the most shocking news he diverted his course, and rushed to his sister's home in great fury. At that moment Fatimah was reading some passage from the Qur'an. She tried to hide that section of the Qur'an as she saw him coming to her but Umar burst into the house without giving them any time and began beating his brother-in-law, his sister too got wounded in an attempt to protect her husband. The blood was oozing from their faces. On seeing these wounds Umar calmed down. He took the text from her and read it himself. He was so greatly moved by these divine words that he asked them to take him to Muhammad immediately for conversion.

As soon as he joined the believers, the community became very strong. He was famed for his bravery, intelligence and was endowed with a towering personality. Although he held no official position, he became the real organizer of the newly formed community of the believer. He became one of the Prophet's chief advisors. His part was in fact more of a councillor than of a soldier, although he did take part in the battles.

Umar was so exceptionally gifted by nature that the power after Abu Bakr naturally passed on to him. Although he was nominated by Abu Bakr, the majority of the companions accepted him as Caliph without any hesitation. He was Caliph from 634-44 A.D.

When Umar Farooq assumed power, the great expansion by conquest had already begun. Umar Farooq himself had contributed to it specially in his capacity as advisor to Abu Bakr.

It is one of his greatest achievements that how he managed to control the fiercely independent Bedouines, executing his plans of expansion so successfully. All the generals were under his full control. One of his uncanny ability lay in recognizing which particular talent lies in different persons. Umar would unmistakably pick up that person and employ him for the job he was best suited for. For example he made maximum use of the Umayyad family in the execution of his plans for the spread of Islam.

During his reign the Muslims, under Khalid the celebrated general conquered Persia, Syria, Palestine and Egypt. In Jerusalem the Christian ruler Sophronius set a condition for surrender— that only if Caliph Umar comes here in person and signs the treaty of peace only then they would surrender. The Caliph therefore set out in 637 for Jerusalem with one servant and a camel. Since there was only one camel he and his servants rode the camel by turns. It happened that on the day they were to reach Jerusalem it was the turn of the servant. The servant insisted on giving his turn to him saying that it will look awkward that the servant is riding and the Caliph leading the Camel. But Umar thought it was not according to the spirit of justice so he refused to do so.

When the Palestinians saw the Caliph of a vast empire in rough, patched cloak, walking on foot with no grain of pride and haughtiness they threw their gates open to welcome him into the Holy City.

Umar Farooq signed the peace treaty with the Christians of Jerusalem, granted them full religious freedom to practise their religion and full state protection.

Umar Farooq adopted the title of *Amir al-Muminin* (Leader of the believers) rather than the *Khalifah Rasul Allah* (deputy of the messenger of God) as Abu Bakr was called. He also instituted the *Hijrah* as the commencement of the Muslim era (622) He instituted *Diwan-e-Ata,* which gave stipends to all Muslims. He founded military centres all like Basra, Kufa, Fustat, which later developed into great cities of Islam. He created the office of Qazi.

Umar Farooq was a political genius and he succeeded in uniting all the disparate elements during his rule. A new Muslim state emerged under his able leadership.

Inspite of being the powerful ruler of an empire he lived an extremely simple life. Because of his high moral character he inspired respect and admiration from all alike. He was at the height of his powers when he was stabbed by Abu Lulu on November 3, 644, a Persian Christian.

Umar Farooq was thus not only a great ruler but also an embodiment of all the virtues of Islam.

USMAN IBN AFFAN – THE THIRD CALIPH (644-656)

Usman belonged to the Umayyad family. He was Abu Bakr's friend and it was Abu Bakr who had introduced Islam to him. Usman accepted Islam without questioning. He was the only member of the Umayyads to become a Muslim during the time of the persecution of Muslims. He was married to the Prophet's daughter Ruqayya. On seeing the enmity of the Quraysh due to his conversion, he asked Prophet's permission to migrate to Abyssinia, the land of the kind Christian king, Najashi. He and his wife Ruqayya were thus among the first to give up their home in the cause of God. When Muslims began to emigrate to Madinah, Uthman too, alongwith his wife, came to Madinah and settled there.

Ruqayya took ill in Madinah and died thereafter. Uthman was very sad. So the Prophet married his second daughter to Uthman. This was a great honour. Uthman came to be known as *"Zun Noorain,"* the possessor of two lights. He acted as the Prophet's messenger during the Hudaybiya peace treaty. Usman was also one of the scribes of the Prophet. He wrote portions of the Qur'an on revelation. He was also one of the ten companions whom the Prophet had given the good news of the kingdom of heaven.

Umar Farooq had nominated a six-man council to choose a Caliph from among its members. These members were. Ali, Usman, Abdur Rahman ibn Auf, Sa'd ibn Abi Waqqas, Zubair ibn Awam, Talha ibn Obaidullah. After great deliberations ultimately Usman was offered the Caliphate. Usman ibn Affan became the third Caliph of Islam.

Usman was born six years after the Prophet and he belonged to the Umayyad tribe of the Quraysh. He was a cloth merchant and was so rich that he was known as Al-Ghani (the rich). Adharbaijan and Armenia were conquered during the rule of Umar Farooq. But after the dismissal of Saad ibn Abi Waqqas' governorship, Adharbaijan revolted. Usman ordered military action against it and the Province was brought again under the Caliphate.

Muawiya, Governor of Syria with the help of Abi Sarah, the Governor of Egypt invaded Cyprus and brought it under Islamic rule. Cyprus served as a military base for the Muslims.

Usman was a simple and kind-hearted man. The administration of a vast empire needed a man of stern character like Umar. Although Usman was a deeply religious man he proved to be a weak leader. His administration was not so disciplined as that of Umar Farooq, the second Caliph. Usman felt that by appointing his friends and relatives to key positions he will be able to probably manage administrative affairs. But this did not happen. Having no fear for being taken to task by the kind hearted Caliph they were all the more emboldened to rule according to their own whims and fancies, without looking after the public good. The public resented such callousness, holding the Caliph responsible for the bad administration. They even demanded his abdication, but the Caliph refused to do so. The Egyptians in particular were angry with him. They blamed the Caliph for replacing a capable governor there with his own cousin who set taxes more than they could bear to pay.

This dissension finally developed into a state of civil war. The Egyptians took more active part in this revolt. The demanded his resignation but Uthman rejected all such advice and preached a public sermon against them. Soon afterwards, while he was at prayer, a group of these unruly men attacked and killed him. He had ruled from 644-656.

Usman's most important contribution to the cause of Islam was the preparation of the second and final version of the Qur'an. He ordered the Qur'an to be written in the Quraysh dialect of Arabia. Then he commanded that a few Copies of it be made and sent to the centers of the Muslim province. Every other version was destroyed, and the Qur'an has remained absolutely unchanged for the centuries.

Ali ibn Abi Talib, cousin and son-in-law of the Prophet of Islam was elected the fourth Caliph. He reigned from 656 to 661.

Ali was a profoundly religious man devoted entirely to the cause of Islam. He was born in Makkah about the year 600 to Abu Talib, chief of the clan of Banu Hashim. Ali was adopted by the Prophet and lived with them in the same house. For, once Makkah suffered from economic depression. Abu Talib, Prophet's uncle had a very large family, therefore the Prophet took into his care Ali, to lighten the burden of Abu Talib.

One day when the Prophet and Khadija were worshipping together, Ali happened to see them kneeling and prostrating themselves and reciting Quranic revelations. Ali found it very strange. He asked the Prophet: "To whom you were prostrating yourself." The Prophet answered. We have prostrated ourselves to God." The Prophet then explained to him about Allah and the revelations he had received. Then the Prophet invited him to worship God alone without associating anyone with him. Ali was excited but thought that he ought to consult his father about it. However he could not wait any longer. The very next morning he came rushing to the Prophet and declared to them his conversion. Saying: 'Allah created me without consulting my father. Why then should I consult him in order to worship Allah.' Ali was the first youth to enter the fold of Islam at the age of 10. He remained a lifelong devoted follower of the Prophet.

On the night of the emigration in 622 it was Ali who risked his life by sleeping in the Prophet's bed at a time when his house was surrounded by blood thirsty men with drawn swords with the plot of assassinating the Prophet. Ali lay there so that the Prophet may leave unnoticed. The Prophet further asked him to stay in Makkah in order to restore all things, entrusted to the Prophet, to their rightful owners in Makkah. Only after carrying out this request of the Prophet Ali left for Madinah. In Madinah Ali married Prophet's daughter Fatima. Two sons, Hasan and Husain were born to them in Madinah.

Ali was extremely brave. He used to display great feats of courage and bravery during the military campaigns. He was also one of the Prophet's scribes. He was chosen by the Prophet for several important missions. After the conquest of Makkah when the Makkans converted to Islam it was Ali who destroyed the idols in the Ka'bah.

Ali was invited by the Muslims of Madinah to accept the Caliphate after the murder of Usman, the third Caliph. For three days after Usman's murder Madina remained completely in the grip of rioters. In such a state of affairs when Ali's name was proposed he refused at first. But the people of Madinah prevailed upon him to give second thought and come forward to serve the people. Ali therefore agreed reluctantly after a long hesitation.

His brief reign was beset by difficulties. The forces of lawlessness had been unleashed. Ali wanted first to concentrate on consolidating his administration and after that to take action against Usman's murderers. He wanted to wait until the conditions were normalized. But the supporters of Usman did not listen to what Ali had to say. They thought that Ali was trying to evade the issue.

The murder of Usman had far reaching effects on Islamic history. The united and determined Muslim community was divided forever. Instead of going out to the frontiers they were involved in internal clashes.

Instead of concentrating on consolidation Ali had to spend all his time in pacifying the warring factions. He did his best to restore peace but he failed to do so without receiving the support of the people.

Ali wanted to base his rule on the Islamic ideals of social justice and equality. But the Quraysh aristocracy of Makkah which had amassed too much wealth in the wake of conquests opposed Ali vehemently. It was this group led by Muawiya that demanded the immediate trial of the murderers of Usman. When Ali failed to meet their demand to bring the murderer to book without delay they revolted against Ali. Aisha, Prophet's wife, Talha, and Zubayr, prominent companions of the Prophet, also took a leading part. This rebellion, known as "the battle of the camel" was suppressed, although after much bloodshed.

Ali had now established himself as caliph by defeating his

rivals. He had shifted the capital from Madinah to Kufah. The first priority in the matters of the state was given to the dismissal of the provincial governors. Muawiya ibn abi Sufiyan, governors of Syria and a relative of Usman too was dismissed. But Muawiya who had established himself securely in Syria did not accept the dismissal order. He came out openly to avenge the martyred caliph. It was an issue on which he could mobilize the support of a great majority of Muslims. He made eloquent speeches to play upon Muslim emotions. He took the stand that since the new Caliph is evading the issue of producing the assassins, which is the demand of justice, the caliph therefore stands disqualified for the office of the caliphate. In this way Muawiya justified his insurrection against the elected caliph.

Muawiya gathered a large army of Syrians while the army of Ali comprised 50,000 Iraqies. The encounter look place on July 28, 657. Malik al Ashtar was commanding Ali's forces. Ali was on the point of victory. But the shrewd Muawiya and his supporter Amr ibn al As managed to avert defeat by proposing arbitration. Ali saw through this trick. But his army forced him to accept the principle of arbitration. This greatly weakened his position.

Then there was another group known as Kharjites (Dissenters). Earlier supporters of Ali, now they turned against him. They maintained that Ali should not have accepted arbitration. They became so deadly against the caliph that anyone who said that he was the follower of the Caliph was mercilessly killed.

Ali inflicted the Kharjites a decisive defeat at Nahrawan. Thousands of them were killed in the battlefield. But this defeat did not end the Kharjite opposition for they were spread out in different parts of the country. The extremist among them preached lawlessness, saying: "All authority belongs to Allah, so there should be no government".

Ali was engaged in extirpating the Kharjites and Muawiya found enough time to increase his influence among the people. Displaying great diplomacy Muawiya managed to cut the ground from under Ali's feet steadily, by adopting an aggressive policy against the Caliph. Ultimately by the end of 600 Ali had lost control of Egypt and Hijaz. His popularity was diminishing day by day.

The forces of Ali and Muawiya met at Siffin. When Muawiya realized that he was going to lose the battle he managed to force the end of the fighting by having pages of the Quran fixed to the lances of his troops. Ali was obliged to accept arbitration. When Ali agreed to this some of his supporters abandoned him. They were not willing to accept compromise and submit the will of God to human judgement. In the months of discussions between the arbiters, Ali's alliance grew weaker. The Kharjites who had revolted against their method of arbitration ultimately decided to assassinate Ali.

Early one morning while he was praying in a mosque at Kufa in Iraq, a Kharjite struck him with a poisoned sword to avenge the men slain at Nahrawan. Two days later Ali died and was buried near Kufah. The most glorious chapter

in the history of Islam came to an end by the death of Ali.

The spot near Kufah known as Mashhad Ali developed into one of the great centres of pilgrimage. Ali's caliphate lasted for four years and nine months. Ali's political discourses, sermons, letters, and sayings collected in a book entitled *Nahj al Balagha* (The Road of Eloquence) are well known in Arabic literature.

According to the famous historian, Philip K Hitti, "Ali dead proved more effective than Ali living. As a canonized martyre he retrieved at once more than he had lost in a lifetime. Though lacking in those traits that constitute a leader and a politician, viz-alertness, foresight, resolution, expediency, he still possessed the qualities of an ideal Arabian. Valiant in battle, wise in counsel, eloquent in speech, true to his friends, magnanimous to his foes, he became both the paragon of Muslim nobility and chivalry."

The Qur'an

The Qur'an a medium-sized book as far as its volume is concerned. It comprises 114 chapters or surahs. The Quran is a revealed book: it is not authored by a human being. It is the actual word of God in human language. The Qur'an began to be revealed to the Prophet Muhammad, upon whom be peace, through the angel Gabriel, in A.D. 610, while the Prophet was sitting in seclusion in the cave of Hira at the top of the Mountain of Light, two miles from Makkah. Thus the scriptures were not revealed in book-form at one point of time. Their various parts were revealed as the occasion demanded. It was later compiled in

Madinah during the last days of the Prophet. The entire revelation was completed over a period of 23 years. The last passage was revealed to the Prophet while he was addressing a gathering at Mount Arafat after performing his last Hajj in A.D. 622.

Since the Qur'an came into existence prior to the era of the press, it could be preserved in only two ways: either by committing the entire text to memory or by writing it on paper or other materials. That is why there have always been a large number of *hafiz* (those who committed the entire Qur'an to memory), in every age right from the moment of revelation of the Qur'an to the present day. The earliest written copies of the Qur'an are still available in different museums, one of these being in Tashkent.

The Qur'an, addressed to mankind, tells us of God's scheme for human existence: that man is placed on this earth for the purpose of being tested. The freedom he is given here is not as a matter of right, but as a matter of trial. On its outcome rests the eternal fate of man. The Qur'an asserts that human beings are eternal creatures, yet only an extremely small part of their lifespan has been assigned to this present world, the remainder ordained for the Hereafter. As we learn from the Qur'an, all the revealed books were sent by God so that man might be informed of the nature of his life.

The teaching of the Qur'an can be summed up under two basic headings: (1) believing in One God and worshipping

Him alone; (2) regarding all human beings as equal and according equal rights to all.

These two kinds of precepts can be expressed as monotheism and justice.

The teachings of the Qur'an can broadly be divided into two parts — abstractions and practicalities. The Qur'an, revealed as circumstances demanded, and not in a purely theoretical way, enshrines only the basic teachings of Islam. The detailed application of these teachings is to be found in the *hadith* (sayings and doings of the Prophet Muhammad).

Regarding social life, the essence of Islamic teaching is that God has granted freedom to everyone. This freedom in itself demands that people should lead their lives with restraint. Because, if freedom is exercised without restraint, it will inevitably result in clash and breakdown, destroying social life in their wake.

The most repeated invocation in the Qur'an is 'In the name of God, the most beneficent the most Merciful. The occurrence of this invocation 114 times in the Qur'an is in itself an indication of how important it is.

Every piece of work must have a beginning. It is the Qur'an's desire that when one initiates any undertaking one should begin by uttering the name of God. One is thus always reminded of God's attributes of benevolence and compassion.

WAHY (REVELATION)

The Qur'an is composed of verbal revelations made to Prophet Muhammad, the Prophet of Islam (one whom be peace) during a period of twenty three years at Makkah (610-622) and Madinah (622-632). The arrangement of the Qur'an is not in accordance with the chronological order of the revelation. The first revelation was verses 2-6 of Chapter 96. The last chapter revealed was chapter 110.

Literal meaning of *wahy* is to intimate or indicate; to communicate; to inspire; to put in somebody's heart or to converse secretly. The basic meaning however of the word *wahy* is to talk to others hiddenly or silently.

The word *wahy* has been used in the Qur'an to express different meanings, for instance it is used to put some message into the heart:

> *We infused this into the (mind of) Musa's mother. (28:7)*

Assignment of duty to both living and non-living things:

> *And thy Lord commanded the Bee to build its cells in the hills. (16:68)*

> *And He assigned to each heaven its duty and command. (41:12)*

To converse silently:

> *Then (Zakariyya) came out from the shrine*

and told them by signs to give glory to their
Lord morning and evening. (19:11)

In the instance mentioned above the word *wahy* is used in its literal sense. But the word *wahy* has been used more often in the Qur'an for the divine revelation made to the prophets:

"*Surely we have revealed* (awhaina) *to thee as we revealed to Noah and the Prophet after him........". (4:163)*

Then we revealed to Musa to strike the Sea with his staff. (7:31)

And we revealed to Noah. (11:36)

FORMS OF REVELATION

The Quran is composed of *wahy matlu*, the recited words, and the traditions *(ahadith)* are composed of *wahy Ghair Matlu*.

The Quran states:

He (Muhammad) does not speak out of his own fancy. This is no other than an inspired revelation. He is taught by one who is mighty in power and vigorous. (53:1)

The external inspiration or *wahy matlu* has been divided into three categories.

1. *Wahy* Quran, that which was given by the mouth of the angel Gabriel and which reached the ear of the Prophet after he knew it that it was Gabriel who spoke to him.

2. *Isharatul Malik*: that which was received from Gabriel, but not by word of mouth. On such occasions the Prophet said: 'The Holy Ghost has breathed into my heart.'

3. *Ilham* or *Wahi Qalbi*: That which was made known to the Prophet by light of prophecy.

Ilham or inspiration of the *sufis* should not be confused with the *ilham* of the Prophets. *Wahy Matlu* is to be recited and forms part of the Quran while wahy *ghair matlu* is the *wahy* which is not meant to be recited. This is preserved in the form of the authentic traditions.

So far as *wahy matlu* is concerned it has reached us without the slightest possible error. The whole of it is preserved in the form of the Quran. But so far as *Wahy Ghair Matlu* is concerned the actual wordings of all the sayings have not been preserved intact.

The following are the different ways through which the revelation came to the holy Prophet. The Quran tells us that God has communicated to his messengers in the following ways:

> *It is not vouchsafed to any man that Allah*
> *should speak to him except by revelation or*

*from behind a veil or through a messenger sent
and authorized by Him to reveal His will.
(42:51)*

Another difference between *wahy matlu* and *wahy ghair*
matlu is as follows:

Wahy ghair matlu is the suggestion thrown by Allah into the
heart or mind of his messengers. The Prophet understands
the substance of the message. It may be a command or
prohibition or an explanation of a truth (a) *wahy matlu* is
the verbal or literal revelation by which the actual words
of God are conveyed to man in human language. This is also
known as *wahy jali* (the apparent revelation). (b) The
second way through which Allah communicates with man
is that He speaks from behind a veil.

3. The third way is through a messenger i.e. the angel
Gabriel brings the revelations to the Holy Prophet.

The following ways of the coming down of revelation have
been mentioned in the Hadith.

1. *Al-Ruya al Sadiqa* (true dreams)

According to a hadith the true dreams are 46th part of
prophethood. Aisha, Prophet's wife has narrated that the
commencement of the divine revelation to the Messenger
of Allah was in the form of true dream which came true as
the dawn of the day.

2. The second way of communication from Allah to Man is

'from behind a veil.' (38:51) Some scholars say that this refers to dreams and visions. Because a certain light is shown in this case which has a deeper meaning than that which appears on the surface. The dreams mentioned in chapter 12 of the Quran are an illustration of this. Through dreams or visions God reveals certain truths.

This also refers to the case of Musa with whom God spoke while He remained invisible to him (20:13)

3. Angel used to suggest directly to the heart of the Prophet, remaining invisible to him. As the Prophet said:

The angel Gabriel has suggested to my heart that none of the living beings would pass away unless he finishes his providence (destined for him in the world).

Sometimes the *wahy* came in the form of the ringing sound of a big bell (*salsalatul jars*). According to a hadith 'sometimes the revelation, comes like the ringing of a bell.' This type of revelation is the hardest of all and when I have grasped what is revealed this condition passes away.

Commenting upon this type of revelation Aisha says: I saw the Prophet receiving revelation on a very cold day and noticed that the sweat was dropping from his forehead. This condition lasted till the revelation was over.

According to the *Sahaba* his body used to become very weighty during such a revelation until the camel on which he was riding used to sit down due to that load.

The Prophet would hang his head and his companions would do the same, and when that condition was over he would raise up his head. Sometimes the Angel came in the form of a man. The angel also visited the Prophet in the shape of Prophet's companion, Dahiya Kalbi.

THE COLLECTION OF THE QUR'AN

The Qur'an is a book of revelations from God. Today it exists in the form of a book consisting of 114 chapters. They were sent down by the angel Gabriel, bit by bit according to the demand of circumstances.

The revelations started in 610 while the Prophet was in seclusion in a cave of *Hira* mountain, two miles from Makkah. The entire revelation was completed over a period of 23 years. The last passage was revealed when the Prophet was addressing a gathering at Mount *Arafat* after performing farewell pilgrimage in A.D. 622.

The Qur'an was not revealed all at one time. It was revealed gradually over a period of twenty three years. When any part of the Qur'an was revealed to the Prophet he used to recite it to his companions. Since the verses of the Qur'an were recited during prayer the companions had to memorize them in order to recite them in their daily prayers.

In this way the memorization and the writing down of the Qur'an both started from the very first day of revelation.

According to traditions, whenever a revelation was received, Prophet called one of his scriber companions and dictated the verses to them. After dictation the Prophet also asked the scriber to read out to him what had been put in writing. This was done in order to correct any mistakes committed while writing.

This was thus the beginning of the compilation of the Qur'an. The next stage after writing down was to memorize the text. Prophet himself asked the companions to memorize the revealed verses and repeat the same in their prayers.

Thus the message of the Qur'an was not transmitted only by oral tradition even during the lifetime of the Prophet. Among his companions were a select group of about half a dozen *katib-e-wahy*—transcribers of the revelations. A few of these scribes were always present and whenever any part of the Qur'an was revealed, the Prophet would recite it to them. Thereupon, at the exact moment of revelation, they would not only commit it to memory, but would write it down on any available material, such as paper, bones, leather or skin. In former times when the accepted way of disseminating the subject matter of a book was to memorize it, then recite it, it was quite exceptional that the Qur'an should have been both memorized and preserved in writing. This was like having a 'double checking' system, whereby memory plus written words and written words plus memory could be constantly checked against each other.

The second point concerns the arrangement of the verses and chapters of the Qur'an. When the Qur'an was revealed in parts, at different times according to the demand of circumstances, how did it come to be arranged in its present form? We find the answer in books of hadith. It has been proved from authentic traditions that the angel Gabriel, who conveyed the revelations of God to the Prophet, had himself arranged these verses. According to the traditions, each year during the month of Ramazan, the angel Gabriel came to the Prophet and recited before him all the Quranic verses revealed up till that time, in the order in which they exist today. And after listening to the recitation by the angel Gabriel, the Prophet repeated the verses in the order in which he had heard them from Gabriel. This dual process has been termed *al-Irza,* 'mutual presentation' in the books of hadith.

It is also established in these books that in the last year of the Prophet's life, when the revelations had been completed, Gabriel came to the Prophet and recited the entire Qur'an in the existing order twice, and similarly the Prophet also recited to Gabriel the entire Qur'an twice. This final presentation is called *al-Arz al-Akhirah* in the books of hadith. (*Fathul Bari*, p. 659-663)

In this way, when by the help of Gabriel the Qur'an was fully arranged, the Prophet recited it to his companions on different occasions in the order with which we are familiar today. In this way the Qur'an was preserved in its present order in the memory of tens of thousands of the companions during the lifetime of the Prophet himself.

In 632 A.D. when the Prophet died at the age of 63 years, the Qur'an existed in two forms: one, in the memory of the several thousand companions, since they repeated the Qur'an daily on different occasions, having learned it by rote in what is now its present order; two, in writing— on pieces of paper and other materials used for writing in those days. These scriptures were preserved by the companions. Although not in their present order, all the parts of the Qur'an existed at that time in written form.

After the death of the Prophet, Abu Bakr Siddiq was appointed the first caliph. It was during his caliphate that the compilation of the Qur'an was carried out. Zaid ibn Thabit, the Prophet's foremost scribe, and an authority on the Qur'an was entrusted with this task. His work was more a process of collection than of compilation. That is, the scattered bits and pieces of the Qur'an in written form were collected by him, not so that they could be assembled and bound in one volume, but so that they could be used to verify the authenticity of the Qur'an as memorized by countless individuals and passed on in oral tradition. Once this exact correspondence between the oral and written forms of the Qur'an had been established beyond any doubt, Zaid proceeded to put the verses of the Qur'an down on paper in their correct order. The volume he produced was then handed over to the caliph, and this remained in the custody of the Prophet's wife, Hafsa. The third caliph

Osman arranged for several copies of this text to be sent to all the states and placed in central mosques where the people could prepare further copies.

In this way the message of the Qur'an spread further and further both through oral tradition and hand written copies until the age of the press dawned. Many printing presses were established in the Muslim world, where the beautiful calligraphy of the scriptures was reproduced after its content had been certified by memorizers of the Qur'an. Thus once again with the help of memorized versions and written texts, correct, authentic copies were prepared; then with the publication of these copies on a large scale, the Qur'an spread all over the world. It is an irrefutable fact that any copy of the Qur'an found in any part of the world at any time will be exactly the same as that handed down to the Muslims by the Prophet in his last days, arranged in the form still extant today.

AL-FATIHA (THE OPENING) AND
THE LAST TEN CHAPTERS OF THE QURAN

> *In the Name of God, the Compassionate, the Merciful.*
>
> *Praise be to Allah, Lord of the Universe, the Compassionate, the merciful Master of the Day of Judgement. You alone we worship, and to You alone we turn for help, Guide us to the straight path. The path of those whom You have favoured, not of those who have incurred Your wrath. Nor of those who are gone astray.*

Man being God's humblest servant it befits him to commence all tasks in the name of Allah, his Creator. He is the source of All Mercy and Compassion. His blessings are continually descending upon all his creation. When we begin any undertaking by taking his name it is as if to pray to the Almighty to come to one's assistance. Who is a being of infinite mercy. If the Almighty blesses any undertaking then it will surely reach a successful conclusion. This invocation serves a two fold purpose; an acknowledgment of our being God's servant, and a divine assurance of success.

God's power and mercy is visible everywhere in the world around us. God has not only created us He has also provided each and everything we require in this world. God has sent us in this meaningful world with a purpose. Besides giving us a conscience to be able to distinguish between right and wrong He has also shown us the right path where truth is distinct from error. He has sent His messengers to guide us along the right path. We have to always remain grateful to God serving Him in full obedience. We have to strive to earn his pleasure and to refrain meticulously from incurring his displeasure. We should keep praying to God Who is the 'Master of the Day of Judgement to have mercy on us to show us the true path; and to help us to avoid the path of those who went astray.

Al Fil (The Elephant) 105

In the Name of God, the Compassionate, the Merciful

Have you not considered how God dealt with the Army of the Elephant? Did He not confound their stratagem and send against them flocks of birds which pelted them with clay-stones, so that they became like the withered stalks of plants which cattle have devoured?

This chapter, comprising five verses, was revealed at Makkah. It takes its title from the reference to the elephants of the army of Abraha, the Christian King of Ethiopia.

Abraha, who ruled Yaman in the 6th century A.D., set out for Makkah with the purpose of destroying the Kabah. He headed an army of sixty thousand men along with one dozen elephants. Tradition says that when Abraha was within a short distance of Makkah, his elephants refused to advance any further. At that point in time, swarms of flying creatures flew over them, showering them with small stones. This caused an epidemic of sores and they fled. Many of them, including Abraha himself, died on the way back. The Kabah was thus saved from destruction by God's special succour.

This incident occurred in A.D. 570, the year of the Prophet Muhammad's birth. This was a sign that whoever set himself against the Prophet or his mission would be destroyed like the army of the elephants.

Quraysh 106

> *In the Name of God, the Compassionate, the Merciful*

> *For the protection of Quraysh: their protection in their summer and winter jouneyings.*

> *Therefore let them worship the Lord of this House who fed them in the days of famine and shielded them from all peril.*

This chapter was revealed at Makkah, where the Quraysh tribe was the custodian of the Kabah. Owing to this position they were held in high esteem throughout Arabia. This gave them a number of privileges. One such privilege was that in an age of general insecurity their trading caravans were not harmed. This special advantage gave the Quraysh a central position in the affairs of the entire region. Their tribe thus became prosperous.

They are reminded in this chapter that, while deriving worldly benefit from being the custodians of the Kabah, they must not forget the responsibilities attaching to this position.

That is to say, they are urged to give a positive response to the call of Truth brought to them by the Prophet Muhammad and surrender to their Creator and Sustainer. By extension, every believer is reminded here to be thankful to the Lord and worship Him.

Al-Ma'un (Alms) 107

> *In the Name of God, the Compassionate, the Merciful*
>
> *Have you thought of him that denies the Last Judgement? It is he who turns away the orphan and has no urge to feed the poor. Woe to those who pray but are heedless in their prayer; who make a show of piety and give no alms to the destitute.*

This chapter contains seven verses. The first half belongs to the early Makkan period and the second half belongs to the Madinan period. The title is derived from verse 7, which refers to those people who fail to offer the least neighbourly help or charity.

This chapter draws our attention to the Day of Judgement, when we shall be held responsible for all our good or bad actions. It also deplores the ways of those who deny the Day of Judgement, treat the helpless with contempt and lead arrogant, selfish lives. They do not extend the slightest courtesy or kindness to their fellow human beings, their hearts being empty of Faith.

The hypocrites may put on a pretence of doing good deeds, but these hollow acts will not avail them. This chapter also warns those who are 'heedless in their prayer.'

Al-Kawthar (Abundance) 108

We have given you abundance. Pray to your
Lord and sacrifice to Him. He that hates you
shall remain childless (i.e., rootless)

This is the shortest chapter in the Qur'an, consisting of only three verses. It was revealed at Makkah. The title is taken from the first verse. Al-Kauthar is the name of a river which flows through paradise, its water being reserved exclusively for God-fearing Muslims. The disbelievers used to taunt the Prophet that he had no son, and therefore he had none to uphold his religion after him. But the Qur'an says that it was in fact the Prophet's opponents who were cut off from all future hope, in this world and the next, while the Prophet was granted abundance by God.

At the time when this chapter was revealed, the Prophet was facing stiff resistance from the Makkan Quraysh. Only a handful of people had responded to his call. At that difficult moment this chapter was a message of hope to the Prophet and to the Muslims.

Al-Kafirun (The Unbelievers) 109

Say: 'Unbelievers, I do not worship what you worship, nor do you worship what I worship. I shall never worship what you worship, nor will you ever worship what I worship. You have your own religion, and I have mine.'

This chapter belongs to the late Makkan period and contains six verses. God asks the Prophet not to force non-believers into the faith. The Prophet's duty was only to bear witness to the truth, spreading the message of God to everyone, without imposing it upon anyone. When, after 13 long years of unremitting efforts, people were not willing to believe, then the Prophet was told by God to say to the unbelievers, 'I do not worship what you worship, nor do you worship what I worship.' After the Prophet had fully conveyed God's message to the people, he was exempted from obligation towards those who rejected his call.

This chapter teaches us to practice tolerance towards non-Muslims and tells us to treat them with respect.

Al-Nasr (Help) 110

> *When God's help and victory come, and you*
> *see men embrace God's faith in multitudes,*
> *give glory to your Lord and seek his pardon.*
> *He is ever disposed to mercy.*

The chapter An-Nasr belongs to the Madinan period and is one of the last revelations of the Qur'an received by the Prophet. The place of its revelation was either the precincts of Makkah at his Farewell Pilgrimage in 10 AH, or Madina soon after his return from the Farewell Pilgrimage.

Allah's special succour always accompanies Dawah, the spreading of the call of truth. The Prophet and his companions made untiring efforts in the path of dawah. Ultimately God's succour came and people began embracing Islam in their thousands. A number of neighbouring countries entered the fold of Islam. However, the victory of believers makes them all the more humble and conscious of their own failings. At such moments the faithful must be overwhelmed with the realization of God's Grace and Mercy. They must attribute all success to the goodness and mercy of Allah.

Al-Lahab (The Flame) 111

> *May the hands of Abu-Lahab perish! May he*
> *himself perish! Nothing shall his wealth and*
> *gains avail him. He shall be burnt in a flaming*

*fire, and his wife, laden with faggots, shall
have a rope of fibre round her neck!*

This chapter was revealed at Makkah and contains five verses. This is the only passage in the Qur'an where an opponent of the Prophet is denounced by name. Abu Lahab, whose real name was Abdul Uzza, was a first cousin of the Prophet's grandfather. He was the only member of the Prophet's clan who bitterly opposed him.

Abu Lahab made it his business to torment the Prophet, and his wife took pleasure in strewing thorn bushes in the path the Prophet was expected to take.

Consumed with grief on seeing many of the Quraysh leaders of the unbelievers killed at Badr, Abu Lahab died a week after Badr. Though this chapter refers, in the first instance, to a particular incident, it carries the general message that cruelty and haughtiness ultimately recoil upon oneself.

Al-Ikhlas (Oneness) 112

*Say: 'God is One, the Eternal God. He begot
none, nor was he begotten. None is equal to
Him.'*

This is an early Makkan chapter, containing only four verses.

The subject of the chapter is monotheism, or the oneness of God. The doctrine of God's pure unity, or the Divine oneness, is clearly stated here: God is not many, He is only one. Everyone is in need of Him, but He is not in need of anyone. He reigns over all things of the heavens and the earth. Unlike human beings, He has no son or father. He is eternal, without beginning or end, and is thus a Unique Being who has no equal.

This chapter has been called the essence of the Qur'an. The Prophet Muhammad once described this chapter as 'equivalent to one-third of the whole of the Qur'an.' (Bukhari, Muslim)

Al-Falaq (Daybreak) 113

> *Say: 'I seek refuge in the Lord of Daybreak from the mischief of His creation; from the mischief of the night when she spreads her darkness; from the mischief of conjuring witches; from the mischief of the envier, when he envies.*

This chapter was revealed at Makkah and contains five verses. It is a prayer for protection. The title of the chapter is derived from verse No. 1, which asks people to seek refuge, in 'the Lord of the Dawn or Daybreak' from every kind of ill arising from outer nature and from the envy and the dark and evil plottings of others.

Since the present world is a place of test and trial, both good and evil will always exist here. The forces of good may be compared to light and those of evil to darkness. The only way, therefore, not to be affected by evils such as envy, magic and sorcery, is by seeking refuge with Almighty Allah. God is the source of all true light, and if we seek Him, we shall be free from all ignorance, superstition, fear, and all kinds of evil. He also has the power to save us from the darkness of evil. Hence the chapter counsels us to have no fear, and after taking the necessary precautions, to put our trust in Allah.

Al-Nas (Men) 114

> Say: 'I seek refuge in the Lord of men, the
> King of men, the God of men, from the
> mischief of the slinking prompter who whispers
> in the hearts of men; both jinn and men.'

This chapter was revealed at Makkah and contains six
verses. Its title is derived from verse no. 1, which counsels
the believers to 'seek refuge with the Lord of mankind.'
This chapter of the Qur'an is a prayer to the Almighty to
grant refuge from the mischief of evil-doers, both human
and occult. In this case, protection is sought especially
from the evil in man's own heart and in the hearts of other
men.

This and the previous chapter are prayers for protection.
The two chapters are known as *al-Muawwadhatayn*, two
entreaties for refuge and protection. The previous chapter
pointed to the necessity of seeking God's protection
against such external factors as might affect an individual.
Here the need of protection from internal factors, that is,
the evil inclinations within man's own self is pointed out.
So long as we put ourselves in God's protection, and trust
in Him, evil cannot touch us in our inner life.

Hadith – Traditions

Hadith meaning a 'statement' or 'report' is used as an Islamic term for the records kept of the words, deeds and sanctions of the Prophet Muhammad. Some scholars have also included in hadith the sayings and doings of the companions of the Prophet.

THE NECESSITY OF HADITH

The hadith provides the second fundamental source of Islam, giving us a full account of the life of the Prophet, and serving as a commentary of the Qur'an.

The Qur'an principally deals with basics. It is the hadith which gives the details and necessary explanations of Quranic injunctions. For instance, the Qur'an says: "Establish the service of worship." But it does not specify how the worship has to be performed. Not even the timings and *raka'a* (units of prayers) are clearly mentioned. We need the traditions to have full information on this.

Even after knowing the details, it may not be possible to follow the divine injunctions contained in the Qur'an. For not everything can be properly understood by words alone. Therefore God's Prophet demonstrated before the faithful how the service of worship was to be performed. He said to the believers: "Look at me, see how I worship, and follow me."

Thus the Prophet, as well as teaching the divine injunctions to the believers theoretically, also put these teachings into practice in all matters pertaining to religion . He himself practised the divine injunctions scrupulously. His practice was not a private matter, it had the status of a detailed interpretation and application of the Qur'an. Once a companion asked the Prophet's wife Aisha about the character of the Prophet. Aisha replied: "He was an embodiment of the Qur'an." The Qur'an repeatedly reminds us of the importance of hadith, enjoining us to strictly follow the Prophet:

"...Obey God and obey the messenger...." (4:58)

"Whatever the messenger gives you, take it and whatever he forbids, abstain from it...." (59:7)

"And, truly, in the messenger of God you have a good example for him who looks to God and the Last Day and remembers God much." (33:21)

The Qur'an thus provides the fundamentals of religion. It is the hadith which furnishes us with the necessary details and explanations. It is as if, the Qur'an is the text, and the Hadith the commentary; the Qur'an being the theory and the Hadith being the practice. Thus the Qur'an and Hadith cannot be separated from one another. They are complementary to each other. Both are equally essential for the establishment of religion.

COMPILATION OF HADITH — A BRIEF HISTORY

The history of the compilation of Hadith may be broadly divided into four stages:

1. The first stage relates to the period of the Prophet till 10 A.H.

2. The second stage is approximately from 11 A.H. to 100 A.H. This is the period of *Sahaba*, the companions of the Prophet.

3. The third stage is from about 101 to nearly 200 A.H. This is the period of the *Tabiun*, the disciples of the companions of the Prophet.

4. The fourth stage is roughly from 200 A.H. to 300 A.H. This is the period of *Taba Tabiun*, the disciples of the disciples.

COMPILATION DURING THE PERIOD OF THE PROPHET

During the life of the Prophet there were no regular compilation of the traditions for they were not generally recorded in writing. However, they were orally transmitted, with great accuracy of detail, thanks to the Arab's exceptionally retentive memories.

1. Some companions had, however, prepared written collections of traditions for their own personal use. Those companions, in particular, who had weaker memories used to write them down for memorization

and preservation. These were also dictated to their disciples.

2. Then there were those companions who had administrative posts arranged for written copies of traditions, so that they might carry out their duties in the true spirit of Islam. Take the case of Amr ibn Hazm. While appointing him as the governor of Yaman the Prophet himself gave him a letter containing the times of prayer, methods of prayer, ablution, booty, taxation, *zakat,* etc.

3. Abdullah ibn Amr ibn al-As, a young Makkan also used to write down all that he heard from the Prophet. He had even asked the Prophet if the could make notes of all that he said. The Prophet replied in the affirmative. Abdullah called this compilation *Sahifah Sadiqa* (the book of the truth). It was later incorporated into the larger collection of Imam Ahmad ibn Hambal.

4. Anas, a young Madinan, was the Prophet's personal attendant. Since Anas remained with the Prophet day and night, he had greater opportunities than the other companions to listen to his words. Anas had written down the traditions in the scrolls. He used to unroll these documents and say: "These are the sayings of the Prophet, which I have noted and then also read out to him to have any mistakes corrected."

5. Ali ibn Abi Talib was one of the scribes of the Prophet. The Prophet once dictated to him and he wrote on a

large piece of parchment on both sides. He also had a *sahifa* (pamphet) from the Prophet which is on *zakat* (the poor due) and *taxes*.

Besides these there were some other documents dictated by the Prophet himself — official letters, missionary letters, treaties of peace and alliance addressed to different tribes— all these were later incorporated into larger collections of hadith.

Compilations of the Time of the Companions of the Prophet.

After the death of the Prophet, interest in Hadith literature increased greatly on two accounts. Firstly the companions who knew Hadith at first hand were gradually passing away. Their number continued to diminish day by day. Therefore, people became more keen to preserve the precious Hadith literature that had been preserved in their memories. Secondly, the number of converts was growing and they showed great eagerness to learn as much traditions as possible.

This was the age of the rightly guided caliphs. In this age the companions had settled in almost all the countries conquered by the Muslims. People flocked to them to hear traditions from them. Thus a number of centres of the learning of traditions came into existence around these companions. When the disciples had learned all the traditions from one companion, he would go to the next companion and so on, collecting as many traditions as possible. The zeal of these disciples was so great that they undertook long journeys to collect traditions from different companions.

In their period there are not many regular compilations. This is the period of collecting traditions. The work of compilation took place on a large scale during the age of *Tabeyin*, the disciples of the disciples.

The age of Tabeyins from 101 to nearly 200 A.H.

This is the age of the followers of the companions of the Prophet. They devoted their entire lives to collecting traditions from different centres of learning. With the result that a large number of traditions were collected. Now it became possible to collect several memories in larger volumes.

Mohd ibn Shihab Al Zuhri is the first regular compiler. He is one of the most distinguished traditionist. Ibn Shihab Zuhri and abu Bakr Al-Hazm were asked by Umar ibn Abdul Aziz, the Umayyad caliph, to prepare a collection of all available traditions. Umar bin Abul Aziz wrote to Abu Bakr Al Hazm, "whatever sayings of the Prophet can be found, write it down, for I fear the loss of knowledge and disappearance of learned me, and do not accept anything but the hadith of the Holy Prophet, and people should make knowledge public."

The compilations made in this period do not exist today independently. These were incorporated into the larger collections of the later period. These collections were not exhaustive works on Hadith. Their nature was that of an individual collection.

After their individual compilations of this period, comes the *Al Muwatta* of Imam Malik (716-795). This was the first regular work which contained well-arranged collection of traditions. The number of the traditions collected by him is put at 1700. After the standard work of *Al-Muwatta* of Imam Malik, following traditionists compiled books on Hadith.

Jame Sufian Thauri

Jame Ibn-Al-Mubarak

Jame Imam Auzai

Jame Ibn Juraij

Kitab al Kharaj by Qazi Abu Yusuf

Kitab al Athar by Imam Muhammad

In this period the traditions of the Prophet, his companions and the decisions / edicts of the Tabiyin were collected together in the same volume. However it was mentioned with each narrations whether it was that of the Prophet, his companions or of the followers.

Third Age of *Taba Tabeyins* (Followers of the Successors)

This is the age of the followers of the companions' successors from 200 to 300 A.H. This is the golden age in Hadis literature.

1. In this age the Prophet's traditions were separated from the reports of the companions and their successors.

2. The authentic traditions were very carefully (and painstakingly sifted from the weak traditions and then these were compiled in book-form.

3. Elaborate rules framed, canons were devised to distinguish the true from the false traditions in accordance with clear principles.

The main attention of scholars who engaged themselves in the critical scrutiny of hadith was given to the recorded chains of witnesses (*isnad*); whether the dates of birth and death and places of residence of witness in different generations were such as to have made it possible for them to meet, and whether they were trustworthy. This activity, to be properly carried out, involved some feelings for the authenticity or plausibility of the text itself; an experienced traditionist would develop a sense of discrimination.

By the use of these criteria the hadith scholars were able to classify them according to their degrees of reliability.

All traditions therefore fall into three general categories: Sahih (*sound*), having a reliable and uninterrupted *isnad* and a *matn* that does not contradict orthodox belief; *hasan* (good) those with an incomplete isnad or with transmitters of questionable authority. *Dhaif* (weak) those whose matn or transmitters are subject to serious criticism.

This is the period in which the author of six authentic collections of traditions were compiled. These works are considered standard works on Hadith, Known as *sihah-e-sittah*, the six correct books.

1. Muhammad b. Ismail al Bukhari, born in 194 and died in 236 A.H. His *Sahih* is next to the Qur'an in authenticity.

2. Muslim bin Qushairi's *Sahih* is the next important work. He was born in 204 A.H. and died in 261 A.H.

3. Ibn Majah compiled the book known as *Sunan*. He was born in 202 and died in 275 A.H.

4. Abu Isa al Tirmizi compiled the book called *Jame*. He was born in 209 A.H. and died in 279 A.H.

5. Abu Abdur Rahman an Nasai compiled his books of traditions called *Sunan*. He was born in 214 and died in 303 A.H.

6. Abu Da'ud wrote *Sunan*. He was born in 202 and died in 275 A.H.

1 (10) According to Abdullah ibn Umar, the Prophet of Islam said: The (real) Muslim is one from whose hands and tongue Muslims are safe. An emigrant is one who refrains from the things held unlawful by God.

2 (12) According to Abdullah ibn Umar, a certain person asked the Prophet which Islam is superior, the Prophet replied: feeding the poor, greeting acquaintances and strangers alike.

3 (13) On the authority of Anas ibn Malik the Prophet said: None of you truly believes until he wishes for his brother what he wishes for himself.

4 (45) According to Abdullah ibn Masood the Prophet said: Abusing a Muslim is sin while killing him is blasphemy.

5 (63) According to Anas, the Prophet said: Adopt ways of ease not difficulty, make people happy, do not turn them away from you in disgust.

6 (41) According to Anas, the Prophet ﷺ said, whosoever said there is no god but Allah and there was a grain of faith in his heart, will escape Hell. One who said the article of *Tawhid* and there was a gain of faith in his heart will not have to stay in Hell.

7 (44)   According to Abu Hurayrah the Prophet said, whoever accompanies a funeral during prayer and burial will receive a reward equal to two *qirat* and the one who returns after the funeral prayer will receive one *qirat*— each *qirat* will equal the mountain of *Uhud*.

8 (46)   According to Ubada ibn Samit as the Prophet was coming out of his home to inform about the *Shab-e-Qadr* he heard two men fighting with each other. Then he addressed his companions in these words "I came to tell you the date of *Shab-e-Qadr* but because of those two men quarrelling knowledge has been taken away from me. Now you should see it on the 25th, 27th, 29th night of Ramazan.

9 (18)   Ubadah ibn Samit has narrated that once some companions were seated around the Prophet. The Prophet addressed them and said: "Swear allegiance to me that you will not associate anyone with God; that you will not commit theft; that you will not kill your children for fear of poverty; that you will not heap calumny (false accusation) on any one, that you will not disobey for doing good deeds; Those of you who act accordingly (who pays heeds to these words) will be rewarded amply by God.

Those who committed any one of these acts, and if he/she is forgiven in this world then he/she will be atoned (expiated for his/her sin) otherwise if God puts a veil over (hides such misdeed) these sins, then He has power to do so. He has the power to forgive or punish. The narrators say that we extended our hand to swear allegiance (to do *bayah*) with the Prophet.

10 (63) Anas, a companion of the Prophet narrated that God said: opt for easier option, do not opt for harder option. Give good tidings to people, do not make them feel disgusted (do not turn them away).

IMAM BUKHARI (810-870)

Muhammad ibn Ismail al Bukhari was born in Bukhara. Bukhari's grandfather Mughira was the first in his family to have converted to Islam from Zoroastrianism. Bukhari's father was a traditionist, but he died when Bukhari was just an infant. After the father's death, Bukhari's mother brought him to Makka from Bukhara.

Bukahri, although physically weak, was endowed by God with great intelligence and a sharp, retentive memory. He was very fond of acquiring knowledge. Being a very devout and religious person, he began to study the hadith at the early age of eleven. He had very soon gathered all the traditions available in Hijaz. Then he undertook journeys for the collection of hadith. He continued to travel for about forty years throughout the Muslim world in the pursuit of knowledge. He went to all the traditionists to gather traditions from them. After having gathered a large number of them, he returned to Nishapur. By this time his fame as a traditionist had spread far and wide. He was therefore given a grand reception by the local residents. Imam Bukhari began teaching the traditions to the people. He wanted to settle down here. But he could not do so, as he had incurred the displeasure of the governor, who wanted Imam Bukhari to come to his palace to give lessons to his sons. Imam Bukhari had refused to do so, for he considered this a degradation of hadith knowledge. Then the governor told Imam Bukhari that his children could go to him, but only if there were no other students present at that time. But Imam Bukhari did not accept even this condition. This enraged the governor, so he gave orders for his extradition from the city. Then Imam Bukhari went to Khartank, a village at Samarkand. There he settled down and died in the year 256/870.

Throughout his life Imam Bukhari was strictly pious, honest and generous to the poor and to students. He did not bear any ill-will towards anybody, not even his enemies.

His entire life and all of his wealth were devoted to the collection of hadith. The greater part of his life was spent in travelling for this purpose. Bukhari began writing very early. He had compiled his first book at the age of 18 when he was in Madina. Afterwards he wrote a number of books. But the most famous and important of all of his books is *Sahih* Bukhari. It is considered by almost all the traditionists to be the most authentic book in Hadith literature. The author himself read it out to 90,000 students. It made his name immortal.

Imam Bukhari devoted the greatest care and attention to this great work. He is said to have got the idea of compiling the *Sahih* from a remark of his teacher, Ishaq ibn Rahwayh (782-852) that he wished that some of the traditionists would compile short but comprehensive books containing only genuine traditions. After hearing these words from his teacher, Al-Bukhari resolved to work at this great task. He devoted his entire life to it. He explored all the traditions known to him and selected only those which were entirely authentic. He collected 600,000 traditions from 1000 shaikhs during sixteen years of hard work. From this collection he selected only 7275 traditions.

Imam Bukhari took such great care in selecting traditions that he used to record each tradition in his book only after ablution and a two rakah prayer. Every tradition was subjected to the closest scrutiny. He accepted a tradition only when he was fully satisfied that all the narrators were completely reliable. He also made it a point to see that all these reporters had met one another. That is, there was proof that one narrator had heard the hadith from another narrator.

Another feature of his collection is that his chapters are arranged according to their subject matter under separate headings. These headings are mostly taken from some verse from the Quran. Sometimes he finds the wording of his heading in the traditions themselves.

As we have seen, the main purpose of Bukhari's quest was to collect only genuine traditions. That is, he wanted to collect only those traditions which were handed down to him on the authority of reliable companions, who were unanimously accepted to be honest and trustworthy. The next most important point in this connection was also to see that these narrators possessed retentive memories. Then the third point to be stressed was that the accounts they gave should not be contradictory to those of other reliable narrators.

He classified these traditions according to subject matter, such as prayer, pilgrimage, jihad, etc., dividing his work into more than 100 books, which are again subdivided into 3450 chapters. Every chapter has a heading. This heading provides the key to the contents of the traditions in that chapter. This has made his *Sahih*, very easy to consult, even for beginners.

Because of all these positive features, the Sahih Al Bukhari has been rightly considered to be an authority next only to the Quran. Many commentaries have appeared in which every aspect of the book has been thoroughly discussed.

"His collection," writes Philip K. Hitti, in his book *History of the Arabs* "has acquired a quasi-sacred character. An oath taken on it is valid, as if taken on the Quran itself. Next to the Quran this is the book that has exerted the greatest influence over the Muslim mind."

IMAM MUSLIM (204-261)

Imam Muslim ibn al Hajjaj of Nishapuri belonged to the Qushayri tribe of Arabia. His tribe played an important part in Islamic history. Many people from his clan were the Prophet's companions.

After the Muslim conquests, many Arab families migrated and settled in the newly conquered provinces. Many members of his tribe held important posts, e.g. Kulthum b. Iyaz was governor of Africa. His forefathers occupied important positions during the time of the four Caliphs. Imam Muslim too inherited a large fortune from his father, who was also a well known traditionist of his time.

Imam Muslim was gifted with great intelligence and a sharp memory. First of all, he studied Arabic literature and other sciences taught in his times. Later on he developed a keen interest in the study of hadith. He began by learning hadith from the great scholars, including Imam Bukhari, who were at that time in Nishapur. This town enjoyed a central place at that time. Afterwards he undertook long journeys to collect traditions from other scholars of repute. He went to most of the important centres of learning in Persia, Mesopotamia, Syria and Egypt, where he attended the lectures of most of the important traditionists of his time, including Ishaq ibn Rahwayh and Imam Ahmad ibn Hambal.

After finishing his studies, he came back to Nishapur and devoted his life to the service of Hadith. He died in 261/

874 on account of having consumed too many dates. One day he was so engrossed in investigating a particular Hadith, that he just did not notice that he had eaten all the dates in the container one by one. Consequently, he took ill and died in 874.

Imam Muslim was of excellent character - honest, truthful and peace-loving. He wrote many books and treatises on Hadith, and other related subjects. The most important of his works is his *Sahih*. Some scholars have regarded it as the best work on the subject. Imam Muslim examined 300,000 traditions before the completion of this book. Out of his large collection he included only 4000 traditions. One great feature of his book is that he selected only those traditions which were free of all defects and were unanimously accepted by the great Hadith scholars.

Imam Muslim strictly observed the principles of the science of hadith. He was even stricter than Imam Bukhari in pointing out the differences between the accounts of various narrators, their character and other details. He shows greater ability in the arrangement of traditions.

Moreover, he wrote a long introduction to his book explaining the principles followed by him as regards the choice of the material for his book.

Thanks to the utmost care having been taken in its completion, the *Sahih* of Imam Muslim has been acknowledged as one the most authentic collections of

traditions after that of *Sahih* al Bukhari. So far as the beauty of its arrangement is concerned, it is held superior to *Sahih* Al Bukhari. Although some scholars, including Imam Nasai, held *Sahih* of Al Muslim superior to *Sahih* al Bukhari, the majority of the scholars have held al Bukhari superior, the main reason being that when Imam Bukhari started working, he had no example before him for such a project. His contribution is very great in that he managed to save all the authentic traditions by collecting them so painstakingly. On the contrary, Imam Muslim had *Sahih* al-Bukhari as an example. He had every opportunity to learn from both its salient features as well as its defects. Imam Muslim himself recognized the superiority of his predecessor.

The *Sahih* of Imam Muslim is regarded as next to *al Bukhari* in accuracy and authenticity. Any tradition which is accepted by both al Bukhari and Muslim has been termed as 'agreed upon'. And these 'agreed upon' traditions are considered to be the most reliable.

Imam Muslim has added to his work an introduction to the science of tradition. His work consists of 52 books dealing with the common subjects of Hadith, such as the five pillars of Islam, marriage, the laws of heredity, war, sacrifice, manners and customs, etc. The book closes with a short chapter on the tafsir (exegesis) of the Quran. The longest chapter is on *Iman* (Belief), which is the opening chapter of Sahih Muslim.

Fiqh – Jurisprudence

Fiqh literally means an understanding and knowledge of something. At more than one place the Qur'an has used the word fiqh in its general sense of 'understanding.' In the early days of Islam the terms *ilm* (knowledge) and *fiqh* were frequently used to denote an understanding of Islam in general. This shows that in the Prophet's time the term *fiqh* was not applied in the legal sense alone. The Prophet once blessed ibn Abbas (d. 68) in these words: '*Allahumma faqqih ho fiddin,*' that is, O God, give him understanding in religion. By these words the Prophet did not mean exclusively knowledge of law. He meant in fact a deeper understanding of religion.

BRIEF HISTORY OF FIQH

After the Prophet, the Companions settled in different parts of the vast Islamic empire. Here they were confronted with new problems, and they had no option but to exercise their personal judgement. The Prophet was no longer amidst them to turn to him for the solution of these problems. Therefore whenever any problem arose they first consulted the Qur'an and *hadith* and only if they failed to find the solution there, they resorted, to the exercise of their personal judgement, while observing fully the spirit of the Qur'an and hadith.

At this stage when the exercise of reason was done to deduce a law, the term *fiqh* came to be frequently used for this endeavour. Towards the end of the first century a movement of collecting hadith started. Large numbers of people devoted their entire lives to collect and record the traditions. Now the knowledge of the traditions came to be termed as *ilm* and the traditionists began to be called *ulama*.

At this stage there was another group who was interested only in those traditions from which some legal rule could be deduced. For this purpose they resorted to the exercise of reason and personal judgement. This knowledge coming from this second group came to be termed as *fiqh* as against *ilm*.

During the age of successors *(Tabiun)* the Arabs settled in different parts of the vast Muslim empire. Consequently they came into contact with different cultures and civilizations—confronting with problems they had never faced before. In their endeavour to solve these problems they made great advances in various fields of learning. Islamic law was also developed as a science. According to Ibn Khaldun the teachers of the Qur'an were no longer called *qurra*, they were rather known as *fuqaha* and *ulama*. Among the successors there were *fuquha* and *ulama*, that is, those who were authorities in law and hadith.

The most well-known scholar of Madina was *Said b-al-Musayyib* (d 94 AH). In this second period of the development of *fiqh* the phrases *ahl al-ilm* and *ahl al-fiqh* were often used interchangeably. *Al-Muwatta* of Imam Malik the most famous book of this period, provides an example when *fiqh* and *hadith* was not yet fully separated. It is neither exclusively on *hadith* nor on *fiqh*. Both these terms were used for those scholars who derived rules from the Qur'an and the *Sunnah*, to give verdicts on legal matters.

Now in the third stage, towards the middle of the second century of Hijrah books, began to be written exclusively on *fiqh*.

During the time of the Prophet there was no such science as that of jurisprudence. The only ideal for them was the conduct of the Prophet. They learnt ablutions, saying prayers, performing Hajj etc by observing the Prophet's actions under his instructions. On occasion, cases were brought to the Prophet for his decision. Prophet's decisions were taken as models for similar decision in similar cases.

The companions occasionally asked him questions relating to certain serious problems, as we learn from the Qur'an the Prophet gave suitable replies to them. People in his lifetime were not interested in unnecessary philosophical discussions or in meticulous details. The Companions generally asked the Prophet very few questions. On one occasion when some person put unnecessary questions to him, the Qur'an asked the companions to desist from doing so. The result was that the Sunnah remained mostly a general directive, interpreted by the early Muslims in different ways. People did not know the details of many a problem even in the lifetime of the Prophet.

Of course the Prophet laid down certain regulations, but the jurist elaborated them with more details. The reason for this further addition to the laws by interpretation is that the Prophet himself had made allowances in his commands. He left many things to the discretion of the community to be decided according to a given situation.

Law was neither inflexible nor so rigidly applied in the

early days of Islam. Different and even contradictory laws relating to many problems could be tolerated on the basis of argument. It seems that the Prophet provided a wide scope for differences by giving instructions of a general nature, or by validating two diverse actions in the same situation. The Prophet aimed at providing opportunities for the employment in diverse circumstances. Had the Prophet laid down specific and rigid rules for each problem the coming generations would have been deprived of exercising reason and framing laws according to the need of the hour.

Hence, in Prophet's times, it was possible for two persons to take different courses in one and the same situation. For example, on the occasion of the battle of Banu Qurayzah, the Prophet sent some of his companions to their territory and asked them to say *Asr* (afternoon) prayers on arrival at their destinations. But it so happened that the time of the prayer came on the way. Therefore some of the companions said their prayers on the way arguing that the Prophet had not meant to postpone the prayers, while others said their prayers on reaching the destination at night-fall, taking the Prophet's command literally. When the incident was reported to the Prophet, he kept silent. The Companions deemed this to be a tacit approval of the actions of both the parties. Had the actions of either party been considered unlawful, it is argued, the Prophet would have pointed out and corrected it.

This example shows that the Prophet while laying down a law, primarily considered the value and spirit of the action and not the form of the action itself. In this case both the parties exhibited their allegiance to God. One of them obeyed the Prophet's command taking it literally and performed Asr prayers at night fall, while the other obeyed him in spirit. This shows that a commandment is not intended per se; what counts is intention and the spirit which constitutes the allegiance to God and the Prophet. This also implies that people can differ in the form of obedience on the basis of interpretation . Hence differences arose in law among the jurists.

After the death of the Prophet the Companions were spread out in different parts of the Muslim world. Most of them came to occupy the positions of intellectual and religious leadership. They were approached by the people of their regions for decisions regarding various problems. They gave their decisions sometimes according to what they had learnt and retained in their memory from the commandments of the Prophet; at other times according to what they understood from the Qur'an and *Sunnah*.

The interpretation of the Qur'an also caused differences of opinions among the Companions. The points on which the Quranic injunctions were either silent or ambiguous were to be explained. The result was that these verses were sometimes interpreted in the light of traditions from the Prophet, and sometimes on the basis of the jurists' opinions. Moreover since traditions themselves were diverse the differences were natural. Sometimes two contradictory traditions were reported from the Prophet. Some Companions followed one, and some followed the other.

In some cases, a Hadith was not known to a Companion; hence he decided the problem on the basis of his own opinion. When the relevant Hadith was brought to his notice, he withdrew his personal judgement. On this account Umar, the second caliph, changed his opinion several times.

On certain occasions it so happened that the relevant Hadith was available but the reporter himself could not understand its real import. Ibn Umar is reported to have narrated a Hadith from the Prophet that a deceased is punished on account of the mourning of his relatives. When

this tradition reached Aisha she rejected it saying that Ibn Umar might have been mistaken or he might have forgotten some relevant part of the tradition. She also observed that the Hadith reported by Ibn Umar goes against the Quranic verse: No soul bears the burden of another.

The Companions, however, tried their best to base their decisions on the Quran and Sunnah. They aspired to keep their decisions and personal judgements as much close to those of the Prophet as possible. Despite their differences, they did not deviate from the spirit of the Qur'an and Hadith.

The Successors took their stand on the opinions expressed by the Companions. They retained in their memory the hadith of the Prophet and the opinions of his Companions. They made attempts to reconcile opposite opinions held by the Companions on many problems. The Successors exercised *ijtihad* in two ways. First, they were not afraid of giving preference to the opinions of one Companion over another and sometimes, even the opinions of a Successor over those of a Companion. Secondly they exercised original thinking themselves. In fact, the real formation of Islamic law starts in more or less professional manner at the hands of the Successors.

With the Successors, the Islamic law began to take its formal shape and develop into an independent subject of study. In this age the principles which governed *fiqh* were the Qur'an, *Sunnah* and *Qiyas* (deductive reasoning). These principles were introduced by the Prophet himself.

Whenever any problem arose the Muslims tried to solve it by first referring to the Qur'an; if no definite answer was found in the Qur'an then they would turn to the *Sunnah*; if there too the problem remained to be solved then they resorted to consensus of the scholars; and as a final recourse they drew an analogy with the Qur'an and *Sunnah*.

Here is an example of how an analogy is drawn. For instance alcoholic beverage is prohibited in the Qur'an, but there is no mention of hard drugs. Since alcohol is prohibited because of its intoxicating effect and since hard drugs generate a similar effect, then by analogy *(qiyas)* hard drugs are also prohibited.

As we have seen above, the science of jurisprudence had come into existence with the advent of Islam, but it developed as a regular discipline in the second century A.H. Abu Hanifa has played the leading role in this gigantic task of compilation and systematization of the Islamic Law.

When after the conquests, and with a large number of converts, Muslims came into contact with different cultures and civilization, they were faced with new situation. To deal with these new situations it became necessary to devise specific rules and detailed directions from the broad principles practised so far. For example, if a person inadvertently omitted some part of the ritual of prayer, the question arose as to whether his prayer was valid or not. It was not practicable to declare everyone of the actions in the prayer as imperative. Therefore the actions were divided into different grades such as *fard, wajib, masnun* and *mustahab*. Differences of opinion arose as regards the criteria to be adopted for this grading. In deciding such questions the scholars took recourse to deduction, analogy and conjecture, in which they followed different method.

The first compilation of *Fiqh* ruling, a short collection in Abraham Nakhai's time consists of *Fatwas* of Ali and Abdullah ibn Masu'd. This was not a systematic compilation. It was in the possession of Hammad who died in 120 AH and was succeeded by Abu Hanifah.

Although by Abu Hanifah's time the accepted rules of *fiqh* had not been collected, they existed in the form of oral traditions. These had not been systematized into a regular discipline. There were no methods of reasoning, no rules for the derivation of orders, no grading of Traditions, and no principles of analogical deduction. *Fiqh* had a long way to go before becoming a system.

IMAM ABU HANIFAH (699-767)

Abu Hanifa An Numan ibn Thabit, a Muslim jurist was born in *Kufah* and died in Baghdad. He has established one of the Islamic schools of jurisprudence.

Kufa the birth-place of Abu Hanifah was an intellectual centre of Iraq. Abu Hanifah belonged to the *mawali*, the non-Arab Muslims who greatly contributed to the intellectual activity in the Muslim empire.

Abu Hanifah came from a family of merchants. So he also took up the silk trade for making his livelihood. He became very well known for his honesty and truthfulness. His goods were very popular in Iraq, Syria, Persia and Arabia. Although his business flourished yet he himself lived a very pious, simple life. A large part of his income was generously donated to charity, helping scholars in particular. Once during his trip he met Imam Sha'bi. Imam enquired of him 'where do you keep moving about." Abu Hanifah replied that his profession was trade so he kept moving for his business activities. Then Imam Sha'bi asked "Do you visit religious scholars". Abu Hanifa replied that he went to them sometimes.

After this encounter with Imam Sha'bi, Abu Hanifah became keen on acquiring religious knowledge. He took more time off from his business activities and devoted himself to the learning of *fiqh* and *Kalam* in particular. His chief teacher of *fiqh* (Islamic Law) was Hammad (d 738). Hammad was the most noted jurist of Iraq of his time. A large number of students came to learn from him the knowledge of *Fiqh*. Abu Hanifah attended his lectures on a regular basis. Due to his sharp mind and memory he very soon acquired expertise in the knowledge of *fiqh*. Imam Hammad was very pleased with him. He was given a special place in his *dars* where the master delivered his lectures. Abu Hanifah remained his disciple for eighteen years. He also learned from several other scholars of repute.

After the death of Imam Hammad, Imam Abu Hanifah was

a natural choice for being his successor. Abu Hanifah had so distinguished himself in his capacity to acquire learning that the disciples did not find any difficulty in the matter of chosing a successor. Imam Abu Hanifah was reluctant to accept this most coveted post. But when the majority of the students expressed their strong desire for Abu Hanifah to become Imam Hammad's successor he finally yielded to their request. Now he came to be acknowledged the head of the Iraqi school of jurisprudence. In his circle there were many promising students like Imam Abu Yusuf, Imam Zafar, Asad bin Umar, etc.

Abu Hanifah's fame spread rapidly. He was acknowledged as a great scholar. His lectures in Kufa were attended by a large number of people. The seekers of knowledge came from far off places with their questions to be answered according to *shariah*.

Imam Abu Hanifah used to solve any legal problem first through the Qur'an. If no specific injunction was available in the Qur'an then he would turn to hadith and the sayings of the Companions. He did not follow the Successors, saying that 'they were men like we are' so we are not bound to follow their decisions. If even after consulting the Qur'an, hadith and the Companions the problem remained to be solved then he attempted to interpret it himself in the light of the Qur'an and hadith. He saw to it that his interpretation did not contradict the commands laid down in the Qur'an and hadith and the traditions of the Companions.

Imam Abu Hanifah was of a very gentle disposition. He was patient, forbearing and of a tolerant nature. He believed in freedom of expression. He never discouraged his disciples to express their viewpoints before him. They also felt free to express themselves before him. They were given so much liberty that his disciples could oppose the viewpoint of their master too. Once a person hurled abuses at him in front of his disciples but the Imam did not react. Maintaining his composure he simply uttered these words of prayer:

> "May Allah broaden my heart for those whose hearts are narrow for me."

Imam Abu Hanifah was a scholar in the real sense of the word. He had fully devoted himself to learning. He had no lust for power. He thought that by accepting positions of power, he will not be able to devote his full attention to learning. Besides he thought that if he accepted a post under the caliphs then he would have no choice but to succumb to their pressure. He wanted Islamic law to develop independent of political authority. That was the reason why when Umar bin Hubair, the Umayyad governor in Kufa, and later on the Caliph Al-Mansur compelled him to accept the office of judge (Head of the Judiciary) he refused. He was even punished, whipped and imprisoned but he did not change his decision.

After he was released he came to Makkah. After some time he went back to Kufa during the rule of Abu Abbas as Saffah. He died in Baghdad in 767.

Abu Hanifa being a merchant had travelled widely. These extensive travels, contacts with great may people of different culture and background, his exposure to varied influence helped to nurture his mind further. Since Iraq was a central place the society here was more advanced than other places. All this greatly contributed to shaping the mind of Abu Hanifa and prepared him for this great gigantic task of development of fiqh into a scientific discipline.

Being a speculating jurist, Abu Hanifah brought about systematic consistencing in legal doctrine. His doctrines are more carefully formulated and systematically consistent.

Before Abu Hanifah's time, doctrines had been formulated mainly in response to actual problems whereas he attempted to solve problems that might arise in future. By the introduction of this method the area of law was considerably enlarged.

His independence, his piety and his selflessness have made him a symbol paragon of Muslim scholarship.

MALIK IBN ANAS (715-795)

Malik ibn Anas Al-Asbahi was born and died in Madinah. He is the founder of the Maliki school of thought. He played an important role in formulating early Islamic legal doctrines.

Imam Malik was a very devout, God-fearing person. He

lived a life of self-denial and abstinence. He often fasted, sometimes about four days in the weak.

Imam Malik belonged to the tribe of Asbah of Yaman, a pure Arab stock. His father Abu Amir was a Companion of the Prophet, and was a religious scholar. Imam Malik also followed in his footsteps. At an early age he had acquired a full knowledge of the Qur'an, Hadith and other religious sciences. He studied with a number of religious scholars of Madinah. He received traditions from Sahl ibn Sa'd, one of the last surviving companions. He also studied with Jafar As-Sadiq, the great scholar of the time. He knew Abu Hanifah, who had also studied in Madinah. He differed from Abu Hanifah on many important questions regarding the authenticity of the Traditions.

Imam Malik was considered to be the most learned man of his time. He was so well-versed in Islamic law that he came to be regarded as an authority in religious matters. His opinions were taken as *ijma* of Madinah. Imam Malik had composed the first systematic work on *fiqh*, that is why people flocked to him, from far and wide, to acquire knowledge from him.

Imam Malik's method in *al-Muwatta* is that on each legal topic he first relates the relevant Hadith from the Prophet, if available, then from some Companion, and lastly the practice and opinions of the scholars of Madinah. Afterwards he states the views of his own school, that is, of the scholars of Madinah, saying that 'so has been the practice since the times of the Prophet in which there is no difference among us.' At times he even rejects a tradition coming from the Prophet in favour of the opinion of a Companion or a successor. For, to Imam Malik the agreed and established practice of Madinah was the ideal practice. People objected to this standpoint adopted by him. But he seems to be justified in his stand, for Madinah enjoyed the position of having an established practice coming down from the Prophet. While other centres were devoid of this distinction. As such those jurists who had settled in Kufa and Basra, for instance, were compelled to lay more emphasis on Hadith instead of insisting on its practice.

Imam Malik's fame had spread far and wide. Once the great Caliph Harun Rashid came to Madinah, there he met Imam Malik and said to him: "O Malik I entreat as a favour that you will come every day to me and my two sons Amin and Mamun, and instruct us in traditional knowledge" Imam Malik replied, "O Khalifa, the science of hadith is of a dignified nature and instead of going to any person, requires that all should come to it."

The Caliph agreed to send both his sons to Imam Malik, who seated them among his other scholars without any distinction.

According to Imam Malik, *Sunnah* does not purely consist of traditions from the Prophet. For him, *Sunnah* is sometimes based on the traditions from the Prophet, sometimes on the behaviour of the Companions and the Successors and occasionally on the practice prevalent among the people of Madinah. Thus, it was the established practice of the Muslims in Madinah which served as the channel to judge the real *Sunnah*.

Imam Malik often refers to this established practice as the consensus of the scholars of Madinah. Al-Shafii, a disciple of Imam Malik, has explained what is meant by *Sunnah* in this context. He says: "You establish the *Sunnah* on a two-fold basis: first, what conforms to the opinion of the Companions, and secondly, which involves no difference of opinion of the people." This makes it clear that by the word *sunnah* Imam Malik means the *Ijma* (agreed practice) of the people of Madinah.

There were about thirty thousand Companions living at Madinah. They had seen the Prophet behave in all sorts of conditions. The Companions were followed by their Followers and they were followed in turn by their Followers. Thus, by the time of the third generation, the *Sunnah* of the Prophet had come to be established in the community.

It is obvious therefore that the established practice of the people of Madinah was far more reliable than an isolated tradition. The Companions and their Followers in general followed the traditions accompanied by practice.

However this does not mean that Imam Malik or his followers rejected all those traditions which were not accompanied by practice. Their stand was to follow the traditions that were practised generally, without discrediting other traditions. Imam Malik observed: "The hadith is there but we do not know what it really means."

We must therefore refrain from concluding that Imam Malik and his followers gave preference to traditions from the Companions over traditions from the Prophet. It was in actual fact not a matter of preferences but it was a matter of the proper channel to approach the ideal sunnah. That is why Imam Malik considers the practice of Madinah as one of the strongest source of law.

Al-Muwatta (The Path Made Smooth) is the chief work of Imam Malik. This book is the basis of the Malikite school of jurisprudence. It deals not only with the sayings of the Prophet, but also with the opinions of several famous jurists of Madinah. It also contains Imam Malik's personal views on various matters of Islamic law.

To Imam Malik the practice of Madinah is the primary source, and *ijma* (consensus) and *ra'y* (opinion) is the secondary source.

Imam Malik has attempted to codify and systematise the customary law of Madinah. The *Muwatta*, being the earliest collection of Hadith and the first book of law, represents the earliest stage of literary development which was common to both fiqh and hadith.

The Maliki school of law is dominant in the Arab west and is also found in southern Egypt and Sudan.

Tasawwuf – Sufism

Sufism places emphasis on the activities of the inner self. While fiqh deals with the performance of external rituals.

The word Sufi is said to have been derived form the Arabic word Safa (Purity). To another group this word has been derived form *Ashabus-Safa* or the people of the bench. With the migration of Muslims from Makkah to Madinah, many Muslims managed to find job to earn their livelihood. But there were some people who had no such worldly engagements. They spent their time in worship. For a living they gathered sticks and they often fed themselves on fallen dates. The Prophet fed them and commanded his companions to do likewise. The Porch of the Masjid where they used to assmble on benches obtained their name.

But with greater certainty the word can be traced to *Suf* (wool). As we know that in the early days of Islam, woolen garments were frequently worn by ascetics. It was a symbol of their voluntary poverty and renunciation of the world and all its pleasures.

The Prophet is said to have received a two fold -revelation, the one embodied in the contents of the Quran, the other within his heart. The Sufism of these early Muslims was characterized by the renunciation of worldly pleasures and an intense fear of Allah and the day of judgements. The early Sufis were strictly speaking ascetics, with poverty as the ideal of their religious life.

Abu Darda, a companion of the Prophet used to say: "If ye knew what ye shall see after death, ye would not eat food nor drink water with any relish; as far myself I wish that I were a tree which is lopped and then devoured."

The outstanding figure in this early ascetic movement was Hasan of Basra. It is said that the fear of God seized him so mightily that "it seemed as though hell-fire had been created for him alone" Gradually the life of seclusion led on to contemplation, and contemplation to vision and ecstasy."

Some Sufis believe in *wahdatul wajud* (the oneness of existence). They believe that the souls of men differ in degree with the divine spirit but not in kind. The human soul is a particle of the divine soul. The spirit of God pervades the universe. It is ever present in His work (that is creative) God alone is perfect benevolence, perfect truth, perfect beauty. Love for Him is true love (*ishq-i-haqiqi*) while love for other objects is illusory love (*ishq-i-majazi*). The beauties of nature are only a faint reflection of His beauty like images in a mirror. The Sufi believe that the real existence is only of mind or spirit. Material substance are just like pictures, leaving no real existence. So we should never attach ourselves to such phantoms but attach ourselves only to God. God truely exists in us as we solely exist in Him. The idea of heavenly beauty is instilled in human beings. In order to find God in all His glory the mystics renounce the world and devote themselves entirely to God. Shariah is the first step that the Sufi has to pass in order to emancipate his soul and be able to join the greater soul.

The Murid (disciple) observes the shariat and the rites of Islam. He makes Shaikh his spiritual guide in the full sense of the word. He always bears his shaikh in mind. He achieves this goal through meditation. Shaikh thus becomes his shield against evil thoughts. Shaikh guards his spirit as his guardian spirit. This stage is called *fana fi ash shaikh* (effacement in the shaikh.)

KHWAJA MOINUDDIN CHISHTI (1142-1236)

Khwaja Moinuddin Chishti was born in Sistan, but was brought up in Khorasan. His father Khwaja Ghyasuddin Hasan died when he was only fifteen years old. After some days his mother Bibi Noor too passed away. Moinuddin was left alone in the world at a time when his native place was being attacked by the Turks. Thousands of people were ruthlessly being massacred. People felt very miserable. The plundering and murdering people was the order of the day. No one could help to save the situation, even Sultan Sanjar was defeated in 536 and he fled from the city.

Orphaned and faced with all these miserable conditions, he was frustrated with life. He felt that the world was a place of vanity. The idea of renunciation of the world came to his mind. It was in this state of mind that one day when he was watering his garden he met a certain Shaikh Ibrahim Qandozi. He was a man of deep spirituality. Khwaja Moinuddin welcomed this traveller into his garden, showing him great respect. He requested him to take a seat under a shady tree. Then he brought a bunch of grapes for him to eat. The holy man was deeply impressed with the spirituality and the sense of service of the young Moinuddin. The saint accepted Moinuddin as his disciple so that he may help him to attain the state of spiritual purity and devotion. The holy man imparted to him spiritual knowledge, and Moinuddin was completely transformed.

Having partaken the taste of spirituality now Moinuddin resolved to renounce all worldly possession. He sold his garden that he had inherited from his father and all other belongings. All the money was distributed among the poor. Now he became a seeker after truth in the full sense. Khwaja Moinuddin now left his hometown for Samarqand. It was a centre of religious education. Here, he received his religious education in *hadith, tafsir, fiqh* and other disciplines. He also learned the Qur'an by heart. He had taken to the path of wandering. After his religious education he now looked for a spiritual guide. For according to *sufi* thought spiritual power can be gained only through personal contact with the *sufi saints*.

During his wanderings to different places he arrived at Harwan near Nishapur. Here he came across Shaikh Usman Harwani, a great saint of his time. He called on the Shaikh and requested him to accept him as his disciple. Khwaja Moinuddin passed through all the vigorous stages of spiritual discipline under the guidance of his spiritual mentor. He attained spiritual heights.

After spending several years with the saint he was appointed as his *Khalifa* and directed to go to India. Travelling through Tabrez, Asfahan, Herat, Sabzwar, Balkh, Ghazni Moinuddin met many saints of that period and visited many shrines in the course of his long journey from Nishapur to Ajmer. In Lahore he spent some time in meditation in Lahore at the tomb of Data Ganj Bakhsh. The people of Lahore wanted the saint to stay here but Khwaja did not accept their offer and set for Delhi.

Although there was a large population of Muslims in India but there was great tension here between Hindus and Muslims. For the Muslims came here as conquerors, to unseat the rulers and to establish their own political domination. Consequently the distance between Hindus and Muslims continued to broaden.

It was only the Sufi Saints like Khwaja Moinuddin Chishti who have played great role in bridging this gap between Hindus and Muslims.

It was perhaps the rampant practice of idolatry which brought Shaikh Moinuddin to India. He thought that India needed guidance more than any other country. Shaikh had passed through so many countries on the way, everywhere people insisted that he should choose to stay there but he did not stay anywhere permanently. His decision to stay in India shows how great was his concern to bring the Indian people to the right path.

Shaikh had halted in Lahore for some time. During his stay he found that there were many religious scholars and spiritual guides in the city. So he set off from there and reached Delhi but here he was all the time surrounded by people. He had not enough time for his devotions so under Divine guidance he moved to the city of Ajmer. He made it his centre of spiritual activities.

There was a dearth of religious scholars in Ajmer. Islam had not yet spread in this distant land. It was therefore in great need to be blessed with the arrival of a Saint like Khwaja Moinuddin.

He arrived in Ajmer in 591 A.H. At that time Raja Pathaura ruled this state. The Shaikh settled in Ajmer along with his disciples. His mission was of love and sympathy, of piety and purity, of equality and brotherhood.

The local people began to flock to him in thousands. His teachings appealed to the core of their heart. When the Shaikh became very popular among the masses Raja Pathaura was alarmed and ordered him to leave Ajmer. The shaikh asked the Raja to give him some time to leave the city. In the meantime Shahabuddin Ghauri invaded Ajmer and defeated Raja Pathaura in 1192.

Shahabuddin had invaded Ajmer earlier but he was defeated. Therefore when he succeeded in defeating the Raja this time people believed that Shahabuddin had succeeded due to the blessings of the Shaikh and that Raja Pathaura was defeated for having incurred the displeasure of the holy saint.

Now after Raja Pathaura was removed from the scene Khwaja sahab received all the opportunity to spread his message far and wide. Now he was no longer a saint of Ajmer instead he became the saint of the whole India. His *Khalifas* (disciples) spread in all parts of the country disseminating his message in every nook and corner of the country.

The great saint died in 1236. Khwaja sahab's contribution to mystic literature is very great. He collected the lectures and discourses of his spiritual guide, Shaikh Usman Harwani.

His tomb is in Ajmer. It is the most celebrated of all the shrines in India. During His *Urs*, the anniversary of his death, Muslims visit the tomb in large numbers from every part of India.

KHWAJA NIZAMUDDIN AULIYA

The real name of Khwaja Nizamuddin Auliya was Muhammad bin Ahmad bin Ali Bukhari. He was born in Badaun in 1236 A.D. His grandparents had come from Bukhara and settled down in India. His father died when he was just five years old. His mother Zulaykha was a very pious lady. It was

owing to her influence that Nizamuddin Auliya reached such spiritual heights.

His mother secured his admission to a madrasa. Here he read the Qur'an and other religious books. Her mother gave him the best education available. After learning the Qur'an by heart, he began his studies in Arabic and Persian languages and in *Fiqh* and Kalam. He worked hard at his studies and very soon he acquired mastery over all of these.

When he was twenty years old his mother took him to Delhi for higher studies. The famous religious scholars of the time, Maulana Shamsuddin and Maulana Kamaluddin taught him theology. He soon acquired a vast knowledge in *Fiqh* and *Kalam*. He gained mastery over logic. He excelled in debate and discussion. For this he came to be called Mulla Nizamuddin Bahhas (the great debater).

But he was not satisfied with his knowledge in theology and logic. His spiritual self yearned for some spiritual saint to show him the path to true spirituality. The knowledge of form (fiqh and theology) did not appeal to him much. He hankered for the knowledge of the spirit (*tasawwuf*) which alone could quench his deep thirst for spirituality.

In the meantime he happened to hear that there lived a spiritual saint in Ajodhan by the name of Baba Farid. So he left for Pakpatan to benefit spiritually from the great Chishti mystic, Khwaja Fariduddin Ganj Shakar. He was warmly welcomed by the saint. Baba Farid placed his own cap on his head symbolizing formal initiation in Chishti order.

By becoming a disciple of Khwaja Shaikh his spiritual qualities—piety, purity, righteousness, devotion— were greatly enhanced. Soon he was so well versed in the mystic path that Baba Fariduddin appointed Nizamuddin Auliya as his *Khalifa* and directed him to go to Delhi. Accordingly, Nizamuddin Auliya came to Delhi and set up a *Khanqah* here.

From his Khanqah he began to disseminate the message of the Chishti order as he had received from Baba Fariduddin. He worked very hard for the expansion of the Chishti order. It was very difficult to go on without seeking any help from the kings and governors but Nizamuddin Auliya's devotion and determination compensated for this. He managed to infuse a new spirit in the organization of the Chishti order. His untiring effort ultimately brought fruit. A large number of *Khanqahs* came into existence. About 700 senior disciples (*Khalifas*) worked in different parts of the country

The most important point that is to be noted is that before Nizamuddin Auliya the emphasis was on individual salvation while now this matter of salvation was turned into a mass movement. This marked the beginning of a new phase in the history of Islamic mysticism. Never before any order had worked for the moral and spiritual regeneration on such a large scale.

Shaikh Nizamuddin settled at Ghiyaspur and planned to spread the Chishti teachings to all sections of people.

Shaikh was very firm and clear that only those disciples who are least interested in government service will be given the *khilafat nama*. These were the basic principles on which the Shaikh organized his *silsila* in Delhi and other places.

These principles shows his deep commitment to human values. These are as follows·

1. The Murids (disciples) must seek the blessing of God through the service of His creatures. Service of mankind was considered by the Shaikh of greater spiritual significance than formal acts of worship.

2. Baba Farid's ideal of love and amity was to inspire the lives of all those who were associated with the order. There was to be no discrimination between one human being and another. All were to be treated as Children of God.

This was a revolutionary concept. Helping one's fellow human beings brought limitless reward. Thus this spiritual movement was turned into humanitarian activity by the Shaikh. The goal before his disciples was to remove sin and suffering from society.

Shaikh Nizamuddin observed that God does not discriminate between one individual and another. The sun gives light and warmth to all people, rich and poor, kings and commoner all. The rains benefit both rich and poor people. Similarly a mystic too must transcend all barriers of cast, creed, colour, language etc., in dealing with human beings — all were equally God's creatures.

Once Shaikh Muinuddin Chishti was asked to explain the highest form of religious devotion which brought man closer to God, he observed:

> *"Develop river-like generosity, sun-like bounty and earth-like hospitality."* (Siyarul Auliya)

Nizamuddin Auliya is known also by the titles of *Mahboob-e-Ilahi*, the Beloved of God, and *Sultanul Aulia*, the king of the saints. He died at the age of 91 and was buried in Delhi.

One of the saint's famous disciples was Amir Khusru, a courtier and a well-known Persian poet. He was so deeply attached to Nizamuddin Auliya that he died in grief in A.D. 1325 at the death of his *pir*.

SHAIKH AHMAD SIRHINDI
(MUJADDID ALF-E-SANI) 1563-1624

Shaikh Ahmad, popularly known as Mujaddid Alf-e-Sani, belonged to the Naqshbandi Order of Sufism. Khwaja Bahauddin Naqshband was the founder of this Order. The first saint of this order to enter India was Khwaja Baqi Billah. He settled in Delhi where he died after three years.

Shaikh Ahmad, disciple and khalifa of Khwaja Baqi Billah, was born in 1563-64 in Sirhind. Shaikh Ahmad's father, Shaikh Abdul Ahmad was a very distinguished Sufi of his time.

In 1598-99 when his father died, Ahmad left his home for making pilgrimage to Mecca. On his way he was introduced to Baqi Billah in Delhi. The saint asked him to stay for a week with him. But soon Ahmad came under his influence and agreed to stay longer. Finally he gave up the idea of making the pilgrimage and became a disciple of Baqi Billah. At the end of two months he was appointed Khalifa by his new *pir* and sent back to Sirhind.

Ahmad was in Lahore when news reached him of the death of his pir, so he hastened to Delhi where he was acknowledged as the head of the Naqshbandi Order. He was soon acclaimed as the much-needed Mujaddid, or reformer of Islam. His fame soon spread far and wide. He not only acted as a *pir* but also purged Islam of numerous heretical teachings which were current among Muslims, much of it was due to the influence of Din-e-Elahi, a religion founded by Emperor Akbar. Ahmad was thus hailed as the Saviour of Islam. His success however was more marked in the reign of Jahangir, when many of the leading officers of the court became his followers. He also managed to effect certain religious reforms among the Emperor's soldiers. Jahangir was so impressed with his saintly life that he became his disciple.

On his advice the Emperor made several changes in matters of state. For instance, the custom of falling prostrate before the king, which had been in force from the time of Akbar, was discontinued. A new mosque was built close to the Diwan-e-Am in the fort, for the special convenience of the king and his courtiers, and the Sunni code was adopted as the law of state.

He thus succeeded, by the grace of God, to extirpate the heresies introduced by Akbar, and purged sufism of many of those un-Islamic elements which had become attached to it through its long history. It was because of his efforts that the doctrines of mysticism were harmonised with the teachings of the Quran and Sunnat. Shaikh Ahmad forbade his disciples to make use of the following practices: the use of music; dancing, while in the state of ecstasy; prostration before one's *pir;* the worship of saints and shrines, and illuminating the tombs of saints.

Shaikh Ahmad is credited with as many as 644 treatises on different religious subjects. His teachings are mainly embodied in a series of letters. Shaikh Ahmad died in 1624 in Sirhind.

Islamic Society

CHILDREN'S DUTIES TO PARENTS

The Qur'an has made it compulsory for the child to treat his parents with all goodness and mercy. God says in the Qur'an:

> *"And your Lord has commanded that you worship none but Him and that you be kind to parents. If either one or both of them reach old age with you, show them sign of impatience nor chide them, but address them in terms of honour, and out of kindness lower to them your wing of humility and say, "My Lord and Sustainer, have mercy on them both as they nurtured, cherished and sustained me in childhood." (17:23-24)*

Thus every adult Muslim must show goodness and mercy to his parents throughout their lives. There is only one exception to this. That is, if the parents ask their children to commit *shirk*, that is, to associate anything with God, then the child is not to obey his parent. In all other cases the children must show love and gratitude to their parents. They must always speak to them gently and respectfully. They must try their best to make them happy, if that does not involve any disobedience to God. The children must take great care not to react to what their parents have to say. If they say or do anything which is not liked or approved of by the children, then they must show patience and tolerance in stead of giving rent to their anger. The children must scrupulously try to refrain from disobeying their parents, since the Prophet of Islam regarded this as one of the major since, next only to it is especially when the parents have grown old that they need great care and attention. Far from showing signs of displeasure, the children must pray for them to God in these words of the Qur'an: "My Lord and Sustainer! Be kind and have mercy on them as they cherished, nurtured and sustained me in childhood."

We must continue praying for them even after they have died. Such prayer will be regarded as a continuous charity (*sadaqa jaria*) as the Prophet has told us.

The children must be more kind and grateful to their mother since she takes greater pains so far as the upbringing of the children are concerned. That is why the Prophet has told us expressly that it is the mother who has the first claim on the child's care and attention.

Once a companion of the Prophet asked him as to whom he should show kindness. The Prophet replied: "Your mother." He asked who came next and the Prophet again replied "Your mother." He asked the Prophet yet again who came next. The Prophet replied, Your mother." When the companion asked for the fourth time, only then did the prophet reply, "Your father."

One of the benefits of being good and kind to parents is that goodness and kindness is passed on from one generation to another. As the Prophet has said:

> "Be good and kind to your parents and your children will be good and kind to you."

THE RIGHTS OF RELATIVES

A Muslim is required to maintain a good relationship with his relatives. According to a saying of the Prophet, we should visit our relatives, inquire about their circumstances, spend on them and give them *sadaqa* (voluntary charity) if they are poor.

According to another *hadith*, if any one of our relatives does not treat us well, even then we have to treat him well. As we know, Islam enjoins us not only to be good to those who are good to us, but also to be good to those who are not good to us. This shows exemplary moral character according to the standard of Islam.

Here are some relevant verses of the Qur'an:

> "Give your relatives their due..." (17:26)

> "Allah commands justice, kindness and giving to near relatives..." (19:90)

> "And show kindness to your parents and to near relatives..." (4:36)

The essence of Islam is thus to serve God and do good to our fellow creatures, including the animals. The worship of Allah is linked up with kindness to parents, kindred, and those in want. It is not a matter of verbal kindness. They have certain rights which must be fulfilled.

From the Qur'an and traditions we find that the institution of the family can only be maintained by feelings of well-wishing and kindness. So the Islamic laws of morality and decency must be observed. If we want to earn God's pleasure and blessings we must abide by the Quranic injunctions, and extend our full support to our relatives.

RIGHTS OF NEIGHBOURS

"Do you know what the rights of neighbours are?" asked the Prophet. And then he went on to give a list:

> *"Help him if he asks for your help.*
>
> *Give him relief if he seeks relief from you.*
>
> *Give him a loan if he needs one.*
>
> *Show him concern if he is distressed.*
>
> *Nurse him when he is ill.*
>
> *Attend his funeral if he dies.*
>
> *Congratulate him if he meets with any good.*
>
> *Sympathise with him if any calamity befalls him."*

This tradition show that we are not only supposed to have good will towards our neighbours but we should also offer practical help whenever they are in need. Nobody can be a believer, said the Prophet, if his neighbours pass the night hungry, while he has his stomach full.

This hadith tells us that nobody can be a true believer unless his neighbours feel secure from his hands and tongue. We are urged to be good and helpful to our neighbours in particular for they, being near, have more right to our goodness and assistance.

Such great emphasis laid by the Prophet on our good treatment of our neighbours shows that the aim of Islam is to awaken the springs of goodness in the human heart. If we can become good to our immediate neighbours, then that will be a guarantee of our being good to others people. For constant good conduct will surely develop a good moral character in us and that will surely reflect in or dealings with whoever we come in contact with.

If we observe the injunction of the Prophet in this matter, then without doubt we shall contribute to strengthening society with the bonds of love, affection and brotherhood.